READING RAY S. ANDERSON

Reading Ray S. Anderson
Theology as Ministry—Ministry as Theology

CHRISTIAN D. KETTLER

☙PICKWICK *Publications* · Eugene, Oregon

READING RAY S. ANDERSON
Theology as Ministry—Ministry as Theology

Copyright © 2010 Christian D. Kettler. All rights reserved. Except for brief quotations in critical publications or reviews, no part of this book may be reproduced in any manner without prior written permission from the publisher. Write: Permissions, Wipf and Stock Publishers, 199 W. 8th Ave., Suite 3, Eugene, OR 97401.

Pickwick Publications
An Imprint of Wipf and Stock Publishers
199 W. 8th Ave., Suite 3
Eugene, OR 97401

www.wipfandstock.com

ISBN 13: 978-1-60899-329-1

Scripture quotations are from the New Revised Standard Version of the Bible, copyright ©1989 the National Council of the Churches of Christ in the USA. Used by permission. All rights reserved.

Cataloguing-in-Publication data:

Kettler, Christian D., 1954–.

    Reading Ray S. Anderson : theology as ministry—ministry as theology/ Christian D. Kettler.

    xxii + 178 p. ; 23 cm. Includes bibliographical references.

    ISBN 13: 978-1-60899-329-1

    1. Theology, Practical. 2. Mission of the church. 3. Pastoral Care. 4. Pastoral counseling. 5. Theological anthropology—Christianity. 5. Christianity—Psychology. 6. Pastoral theology. I. Anderson, Ray Sherman. II. Title.

BV4011.3 K48 2010

Manufactured in the U.S.A.

For my friend—and Ray's friend—Todd Speidell

CONTENTS

Preface / ix
Abbreviations of Books by Ray S. Anderson / xx

I. ON THEOLOGY AS MINISTRY

1. "Exploration into God": The Doctrine of God and God's Ministry / 3
2. On Being Human: Theological Anthropology and the Humanity of God / 25
3. Jesus Christ, Divine Reconciliation, and the Healing of Persons / 58

II. ON MINISTRY AS THEOLOGY

4. Ministry as the Real Presence of Christ: A Sacramental and Relational Reality / 95
5. Ministry and Mission: Community as Kenotic and Ek-static / 123
6. Ministry as the Future of Christ in the Kingdom of God / 150

Bibliography / 175

PREFACE

THERE IS A simple reason for this book: to encourage more people to read Ray S. Anderson (1925–2009). For many years Professor of Theology and Ministry at Fuller Theological Seminary, Anderson was a theologian who never ceased to be a pastor. Whether you are a clergy person or a lay person, whatever your denomination or Christian heritage may be, Ray Anderson has many exciting, and sometimes provocative, things to say. I speak from experience as a student of Anderson's, beginning at Fuller Seminary, but extending along many years. While reading almost any of his many books, I am always struck by both a depth of insight and an almost joyful playfulness for the ministry of theology. That is why the subtitle of the book expresses the dialectic that is always maintained in Anderson's thought: Theology is ministry itself, a ministry of meditating upon the gospel of the unconditional grace of God in Jesus Christ, but ministry itself is also theology; true ministry, the ministry of God, always precedes and governs theology.[1] More on that later.

For over thirty years, Ray Anderson quietly wrote a body of work that is remarkable in its ability to awaken both the academy and the church to a theology that actually intersects with the ministry of the church and a view of ministry that dwells in a deep place of reflection. My purpose is to introduce the reader to some of Anderson's seminal insights, with only a few critical responses. My regret is that I will be unable to replicate the spark of playfulness and intellectual restlessness that characterized Anderson's writings, lectures, and sermons. Donald Mackinnon, the noted Cambridge

---

1. Anderson, "A Theology for Ministry," 7, 20.

theologian who has received new interest in recent years, spoke of this "nervous, restless quality" even in Anderson's doctoral dissertation (later published as *Historical Transcendence and the Reality of God*).[2] Anderson's lectures were for many years a refuge of grace for weary students who were bounced back and forth in seminary classes, from studying academic, critical disciplines in one to learning pastoral and ministry skills in another, with little integration of the two. Most of all, in the midst of personal crises, the students found in Anderson's lectures (and pastoral counsel) grace to help in time of need (Heb 4:16). Unconditional grace was not just a doctrine for Anderson, but the way that he responded to people, even in their weaker moments. For what Anderson meant by a theology of ministry was not simply a thin veneer of Bible verses justifying the typical, prosaic ministry program of a congregation. Rather, his theology of ministry was truly *incarnational*, the Word penetrating deeply into our flesh (John 1:14), the flesh of the whole person, involving spiritual, emotional, and physical turmoils. That is where Jesus Christ meets us, and continues to meet us, not in a ministry of our own creation, but in participating in his continuing ministry, *God's ministry*.

In recent years Anderson found more dialogue with Christian psychologists than theologians (perhaps attesting to a fear among theologians of their own humanity?). This bore fruit in a remarkable issue of *Edification: Journal of the Society for Christian Psychology*, in which Anderson's article "Toward a Holistic Psychology: Putting all the Pieces in their Proper Place" was followed by several responses from psychologists, philosophers, and theologians.[3] This kind of critical interaction, certainly not uncritical, demonstrates the stimulation that Anderson's thought can provide for all three groups of scholars whilst at the same time benefitting all of those involved in the ministry of Jesus Christ.

For all of Anderson's commitment to community there was a freedom in his theology to be a maverick, to be oneself, and go against the grain. J. G. Hamann and Dag Hammarskjöld are two iconoclasts he liked to quote. Anderson presented an interesting portrait of the maverick theologian in the midst of community; not an easy venture, as his former colleagues and students will attest!

2. Foreword by Donald Mackinnon in Anderson, *Historical Transcendence and the Reality of God*, ix.

3. Anderson, "Toward a Holistic Psychology." Cf. Young, "The Ontological Self in the Thinking of C. Stephen Evans and Ray S. Anderson."

Preface

I have to admit that re-reading Anderson's work and appreciating afresh the depth and perception of his theology seems to make this book what I have laughingly called to my friends, "Ray-Lite." Good theology is not just a display of erudition, as Thomas Torrance told me once. Ray Anderson is not a historical theologian, biblical scholar, or philosopher in the guise of a theologian. Unapologetically, he is a "restless" theologian in service to the church of Jesus Christ. Good theology is being faithful to Jesus Christ and demonstrating that faithfulness with the kind of "nervous, restless quality" of mind that Donald Mackinnon spoke of Anderson's thought. But Anderson is doubly challenging in that he refuses to allow for a theology that does not partake, like the incarnation, of actual human flesh; the human flesh of human dilemmas, perplexities, and ambiguity. I remember well Ray Anderson telling a class that one must always be open to a "doctrine of ambiguity." How difficult was it for us conservative evangelical students to hear that! But we came to realize that the ambiguity rightly exists in our limited and fallen understandings, not in God.

This book is not a scholarly study of Ray Anderson, in the sense of exploring his influences and critically debating his place in the history of contemporary theology. I hope this book will inspire others to do that. The intellectual influences on Anderson were many and profound, including Edward Carnell, Kierkegaard, the philosopher John Macmurray, Karl Barth, Dietrich Bonhoeffer, Thomas Torrance, James Torrance, and the interdisciplinary work of Ernest Becker—*The Denial of Death*. Ray Anderson was probably the first English-speaking theologian (in his dissertation published in 1975) to recognize the profound theological anthropology and ecclesiology in the work of the Greek Orthodox theologian John Zizioulas. Anderson provided an interesting case study of American evangelicalism in the mid-twentieth century when some were trying to provide an intellectual alternative not only to fundamentalism but also to the rationalistic theology that was presented by such early Fuller Seminary professors like Carl F. H. Henry. Anderson's critique of Henry is very telling and insightful.[4] Such an exhaustive and in-depth study of Anderson would be a very admirable project, but this book is not it. Its aim is more modest; to provide an entrée point into the fascinating riches of Anderson's theological "musings"—the musings of "a maverick

---

4. Anderson, "Carl F. H. Henry: 'Evangelical Theologian.'"

theologian," as he liked to put it. His place, and often a controversial place in the modern history of Fuller Seminary and modern evangelicalism, is a topic worthy of further study.[5] My aim is more modest, but I think, important. "Reading Ray" is an experience!

One will be struck with the sheer *humanity* of Anderson's theology. The incarnation is not just an orthodox or abstract doctrine for him. I have two "Rays" that have been very influential on my life and thought: Ray Anderson and the fantasy writer Ray Bradbury, author of *Fahrenheit 451* and *The Martian Chronicles*. Bradbury's writings have a profound humanity yet always with a sense of wonder and respect for the divine. In a way, as Ray Bradbury has brought a sense of God in the humanity of fantasy and science fiction writing, Ray Anderson has brought a sense of humanity into God in the field of theology. Anderson's writings have that same respect for humanity that Bradbury's do for the divine.

I must admit that this discussion of Ray Anderson is a personal one that includes what I think is most important in Anderson's theology. Because Anderson is rare among theologians in that he hits the reader in a very personal way, these emphases reflect my own interests (and sometimes pathologies!) and are not meant to say that others (including Ray!) might find different gems of ideas and streams of thinking more profitable. Of necessity, I have had to leave out much that might prove to be fruitful for another reader. This is just another way to say, "Dig into Anderson!"

---

5. See Richard Mouw's, Colin Brown's and Richard Muller's less than enthusiastic comments about the Barth centennial in 1986 ("Now That the Party Is Over Was Karl Barth That Good?"), and Ray Anderson's satirical response to their criticisms in the same journal, 37.5 (1987) 6–8. Anderson once said that criticisms of Barth are easy, like shooting an elephant; you're bound to hit something! The contribution of Anderson to evangelicals' reevaluation of Barth is discussed in Phillip R. Thorne, *Evangelicalism and Karl Barth*, 117–23. Cf. John P. Lewis, "The Formative Influence of Karl Barth in the Theology of Ray S. Anderson," and Lewis, *Karl Barth in North America*. Anderson was included in the "notorious" company of those attacked by Harold Lindsell in "the battle of the Bible" debate over biblical inerrancy in the 1970s, as found in Harold Lindsell, *The Bible in the Balance*. Lindsell bizarrely speaks of Anderson's view as God as a Kantian agnosticism! A more positive response to Anderson on transcendence is found in Kenneth Surin, *The Turnings of Darkness and Light*, 186–89. See also "Foreword: An Appreciation" by Kenneth Surin in, *On Being Christian . . . and Human*, 6–8. Surin relates that it was the current Archbishop of Canterbury, Rowan Williams, who first led him to Anderson's *Historical Transcendence and the Reality of God*. Williams' review of that book is found in the *Downside Review* 94.316 (1976) 236–39.

Preface

Born on a South Dakota farm, Ray Anderson came from the soil of the very human and practical endeavor of the farmer and transplanted that humanity into the struggles of American evangelicalism as a pastor, and student and teacher at Fuller Theological Seminary. While a young farmer himself, Anderson listened to one of the most successful of the early radio evangelists, Charles E. Fuller, and his radio program, "The Old Fashioned Revival Hour." From then, Anderson and his family travelled to Pasadena, California to enroll in Fuller's relatively new theological seminary. The young Anderson found a form of the traditional American revivalistic tradition that had become preoccupied with correcting its intellectual and cultural deficiencies, now calling itself, "evangelicalism." These sons (at that time almost exclusively male) of evangelists sought to avoid the parochialism and obscurantism of their fundamentalist forebears while holding fast to what they perceived to be the eternal faith. The influence of Edward J. Carnell, a restless, iconoclastic, and troubled evangelical mind and professor at Fuller Seminary, was a great stimulation to the young farmer turned seminary student to move beyond simply regurgitating the new "evangelicalism."

Planting a new Evangelical Free Church congregation in Covina, California exposed Anderson to the very real experience of a young pastor. "Restless" is the word that seems to have continued to characterize Ray Anderson in his early days in pastoral ministry. During this time of living with the raw realities of a congregation and the stereotypical expectations of a "reverend," Anderson found himself jotting down short "musings" as he would later call them—a theological notebook of the daring of faith that sought to think beyond the stereotypes of ministry and theology. Published much later as *Soulprints* (1996), this theology in the midst of ministry was to be hashed out in the context of the increasingly alienated culture of the 1960s. The result was a ministry that sought consciously to be incarnational, less concerned with success than with human beings trapped in an alienating world.[6]

Mid-life took Anderson to Scotland to study for a PhD in theology at the University of Edinburgh under the noted theologian Thomas F. Torrance. Torrance, a student of Karl Barth's, provided for Anderson a theology that would put words to what he had begun to experience in

---

6. A series of lively messages on the statement of faith of the Evangelical Free Church was published in 1964 while Anderson was a pastor in Covina, California, titled *Like Living Stones*.

Preface

Covina: an incarnational ministry that drove one to ask new questions of God. The result was his doctoral dissertation, *Historical Transcendence and the Reality of God*, published in 1975. Borrowing deeply from Dietrich Bonhoeffer, John Macmurray, and Ronald Gregor Smith, Anderson sought to orient the doctrine of God in an increasingly skeptical age to a view of transcendence that is not "other-worldly," but based on the incarnation of God in Jesus Christ. A strikingly original ecclesiology proceeded from this, Anderson's first major theological work.

After a short time teaching at Westmont College in California, Ray Anderson joined the faculty of Fuller Theological Seminary in 1976. As theological mentor for Fuller Seminary's growing Doctor of Ministry program, Anderson assembled the massive anthology, *Theological Foundations for Ministry* (1979). Not content with simply gathering a plethora of competing theologies for the student to be befuddled by, Anderson presented a coherent theology based on the Trinity and the incarnation, including generous selections from Barth, Bonhoeffer, Thomas and James Torrance, and others including the most ecclesiologically dynamic sections of *Historical Transcendence and the Reality of God*. Of special note is the essay by Anderson, "A Theology of Ministry," in which he laid out the significance of ministry preceding and governing theology—rather than ministry as the opposite of theology—based on an incarnational theology in which God is "on both sides" of both revelation and reconciliation. Reconciliation, like all of God's ministry, is not to be left up to us! Such an anthology signaled to many that a new way of integrating theology and ministry was being proposed that did not simply try to find a lowest common denominator in ethical values or pastoral practice, but was based on the richness of the triune life of God revealed in Jesus Christ. This was a different kind of evangelical theology than the apologetics-driven heritage of the early Fuller Seminary, but one which was just as loyal to the ancient faith in the Trinity and the incarnation. Yet it was refreshingly free to acknowledge not just that Jesus Christ was God, but that God actually assumed human flesh, so an incarnational theology and ministry is not afraid but embraces the human, as messy as that might often be in the realities of ministry.

The incarnational imperative of a humanizing theology (including in the church!) drove Anderson increasingly into questions of a theological anthropology. Questions of theological anthropology had begun to intrigue Anderson when he observed how little theological basis there existed with some colleagues at Westmont, whom otherwise possessed a strong, personally pious theology, yet seemed often to offer little integration with their academic disciplines. His pious colleagues seemed to be operating with more of a philosophical, non-theological anthropology than one that was rooted in the incarnation. The fruit of Anderson's thinking came in 1982 with the publication of *On Being Human: Essays in Theological Anthropology*. I don't think that Karl Barth's profound writings on the doctrine of humanity had ever been mined so thoroughly in light of pastoral and ministry practice. Yet Anderson remained very much his own man. As a seminarian at the time, I remember vividly the excitement of Anderson's terse yet provocative prose, bursting with genuine theological and ministerial potential. Not easy to digest for some, but for many, Anderson's continuing "nervous, restless quality" was the stimulation to believe in the continued healing power of a trinitarian-incarnational theology, the healing power of the living, triune God. Many a Fuller Seminary student can attest to practically stumbling into a Ray Anderson class week upon week, beaten up by life's events, desperately seeking the grace of God . . . and finding it in Ray's provocative and faithful witness to Jesus Christ.

On Being Human only served to further ignite Anderson's creative theological fire, particularly in the implications of a theological anthropology. Anderson's theological anthropology is profoundly relational, including male and female relationships and the family, so it was natural that *On Being Family: A Social Theology of the Family*, written with the family sociologist Dennis B. Guernsey, and the fruit of their team-taught course at Fuller, "Theology and Ecology of the Family," was published in 1984. The provocative and pastoral thinking on death and dying in *On Being Human* led to *Theology, Death and Dying* in 1986. Anderson was fond of mischievously suggesting that he wanted the book to be entitled, *On Being Dead*, in order to harmonize with *On Being Human* and *On Being Family*, and perhaps to include ethics and be called, *On Being Good and Dead!*

Anderson's integrative interests continued to be broad and sweeping with the volume on leadership, *Minding God's Business*, in 1986 and one on counseling, *Christians Who Counsel*, in 1990. No shoddy thinking here, Anderson demonstrated his theological bravery in taking on such "nuts and bolts" issues of ministry.

In 1991, Anderson wrote his first "popular" book, but one that is truly profound in its thinking: *The Gospel According to Judas: Is There a Limit to God's Forgiveness?* Featuring an imaginary conversation between Jesus and Judas after Judas' death, this book has deeply affected and challenged many regarding how shallow our view of grace and forgiveness often is. Still, many have been offended, even with the later version, *Judas and Jesus: Amazing Grace for the Wounded Soul* (2005). These little books still continue to have a great ministry, even including, as Anderson related, with a convicted murderer serving life in prison. Concern for the individual desperately needing the grace of God is evident in many of Anderson's later books such as, *Don't Give Up On Me—I'm Not Finished Yet! Putting the Finishing Touches on the Person You Want to Be* (1994), and its more technical cousin, *Self-Care: A Theology of Personal Empowerment and Spiritual Healing* (1995), *Living the Spiritually Balanced Life: Acquiring the Virtues You Admire* (1998), *Everything That Makes Me Happy I Learned When I Grew Up* (1995), *Unspoken Wisdom: Truths My Father Taught Me* (1995), *Exploration Into God: Sermonic Meditations on the Book of Ecclesiastes* (2006), and *The Seasons of Hope: Empowering Faith Through the Practice of Hope* (2008).

The church, the corporate, communal, and relational nature of the Christian life, and the presence of Christ today, however, were never far from Anderson's thought and pen. *Ministry on the Fireline: A Practical Theology for an Empowered Church* (1993) challenged an evangelical theology which emphasizes a "Word" theology to embrace as well a "Spirit" or "Pentecostal" theology of the presence of the Holy Spirit in mission. Such concerns continued with what was the summary of decades of Ray Anderson's thinking on a theology of ministry based on a trinitarian-incarnational theology: *The Soul of Ministry: Forming Leaders for God's People* (1997). Wide-ranging concerns from homosexuality to "The Humanity of God in the Soul of the City" are developed in light of a trinitarian model of practical theology in *The Shape of Practical Theology: Empowering Ministry with Theological Praxis* (2001). Anderson's disgust with the lack of practical ecclesiology in much of modern systematic theology reflected his desire to leave "systematic theology" behind for the sake of "practical theology." This direction from systematic to practical theology was spelled out more in theological detail in *The Soul of God: A Theological Memoir* (2004). Anderson continued to provoke his evangelical roots (and colleagues!) with *Dancing with Wolves While Feeding the Sheep: The Musings of a Maverick Theologian* (2001) with such chapters as, "Was Jesus an Evangelical?" (the "wolves" were his faculty colleagues!).

Preface

One of Anderson's most challenging proposals was his practical theology for secular caregivers found in *Spiritual Caregiving as Secular Sacrament: A Practical Theology for Professional Caregivers* (2003). One of his last works provided a theological challenge to and resource for the Emerging Church movement: *An Emerging Theology for Emerging Churches* (2006).

There are many treasures of ideas in all of these books, ideas that have been much appreciated by colleagues and students alike through the years. Much critical thinking stimulated by Ray Anderson's theology can be found in the two *Festschriften* edited in honor of Ray: *Incarnational Ministry: The Presence of Christ in Church, Society, and Family: Essays in Honor of Ray S. Anderson* (edited by Christian D. Kettler and Todd H. Speidell, 1990), including essays by Thomas Torrance, James Torrance, Geoffrey Bromiley, Colin Gunton, Alan Lewis, and Lewis Smedes (with a telling introduction by the president of Fuller Seminary, David Allan Hubbard and a bibliography through 1990) and *On Being Christian . . . and Human: Essays in Celebration of Ray S. Anderson* (edited by Todd H. Speidell, 2002), which includes contributions from many of Ray's former students, including LeRon Shults and Willie Jennings and an essay on "Community in the Life and Theology of Ray Anderson" by Daniel Price (along with a bibliography through 2002). Also included are the case studies used by Anderson for many years in his theology sequence of courses.

Karl Barth, in the lectures he gave during his tour of the United States late in his life, remarked that what he desired for Americans was to be freed for a "theology of freedom."[7] In a way, I think Ray Anderson was the purest example of an answer to Barth's desire for America: A theologian who was always first of all a pastor of a concrete, local church, never deserting the church for the rarified air of seclusion in the academy, never deserting particular, actual people for abstract values or virtues. For most of Ray's more than twenty years of seminary teaching he was preaching every week at what he called, with a twinkle in his eye, the "high of the low churches," Harbour Fellowship in Huntington Beach, California. Anderson built upon Barth's revolution but was distinctly a theologian for the church in the contemporary U.S. Much is made today of a need for a theology of "globalization" and "postmodernism" and certainly the church and the gospel are for the world. But Anderson's roots in a South Dakota farm and an evangelical parish became real in a theology that

---

7. Barth, *Evangelical Theology*, xii.

Preface

took very seriously actual human beings and concrete situations in the church, not to be swallowed up by what can become abstract ideals and causes, from orthodoxy to social justice.

My attempt to organize some of Anderson's many themes is pedagogical and theological: "Theology as Ministry" particularly relates to the doctrines of God and theological anthropology. "Ministry as Theology" suggests his profound integration of theology and *praxis* for the church in its ministry and mission. But the dialectical aspect of "Theology as Ministry, Ministry as Theology" should not be forgotten. There is one ministry of God, Anderson contends, the ministry of Jesus Christ. Theology only seeks to serve that ministry. Anderson was well known for his use of case studies in exploring the implications of theology in ministry. (The actual cases he uses for examinations in his courses are found in the second *Festschrift, On Being Christian . . . and Human*, edited by Todd Speidell). So at the end of each chapter I have included a case that "fleshes out" the implications of that chapter for ministry. (My thanks to Marcia Dillon, Joe Barthell, Randy Myers, Derek Maris, Laurinda Wade, graduate students at Friends University, and an anonymous pastor for the "Visitors to Church" case study, for providing the case studies.) I think you will find that the writings of Ray Anderson will be an incredible stimulation to your participation in the ministry of Jesus Christ.

The preface appeared in an abridged form as a eulogy for Ray Anderson in "Faith and Theology," the blog of Benjamin Myers, Lecturer in Systematic Theology at Charles Sturt University in Sydney, Australia (http://faith-theology.blogspot.com/) and is reproduced with permission.

My thanks to Jollene Anderson and the Anderson family for permission to reprint charts from Ray's books, and their support for this endeavor.

I am grateful to the trustees and administration of Friends University for the sabbatical granted in the spring 2009 semester in order to complete this work.

The students in my Fall, 2009 "Theology of Ministry" graduate course at Friends University, David Benavides, Amy Claassen, Abbey Dohm, Dennis Gill, Beverly Herron, Ken Hultmann, Dionte Johnson, Jesse Penna, Darrel Sears, Wes Smothermon, Cynthia Twillman, and Craig Willet, read through this book with me, providing a theological and pastoral sounding board for which I am very grateful.

Preface

It was a pleasure as usual to work with Robin Parry, Kristen Bareman, and the fine people at Pickwick Publications and Wipf and Stock Publishers.

Assistance provided by my student assistants, Audrey Wade and Kara Yuza, was much appreciated. My friend Erin Doom took time out of writing his doctoral dissertation and busy schedule to proofread the book, providing an invaluable service.

This book is dedicated to my friend Todd Speidell, with whom I have wrestled with Ray Anderson's theology for over thirty years, in a PhD program under Anderson, and in the midst of life with its sorrows and joys. He has been a great gift to me of what Karl Barth and Ray Anderson speak of as the essence of being human: "co-humanity."

ABBREVIATIONS

Books by Ray S. Anderson (with annotations)

CWC   *Christians Who Counsel: The Vocation of Wholistic Therapy.* Grand Rapids: Zondervan, 1990. Argues for a distinction between "Christians who counsel" and "Christian counseling."

DGU   *Don't Give Up On Me—I'm Not Finished Yet: Putting the Finishing Touches on the Person You Want to Be.* New York: McCracken, 1994. A popular version of *Self-Care*.

DWW   *Dancing with Wolves while Feeding the Sheep: Musings of a Maverick Theologian.* Reprint. Eugene, OR: Wipf and Stock, 2002. Unique answers to provocative theological and pastoral questions, such as "Does Jesus think about things today?" and "What do I say at the graveside of a suicide?"

ETEC   *An Emerging Theology for an Emerging Church.* Downers Grove, IL: InterVarsity, 2006. A dialogue with the Emerging Church movement.

ETMM   *Everything That Makes Me Happy I Learned When I Grew Up.* Downers Grove, IL: InterVarsity. On the nature of happiness.

EIG   *Exploration into God: Sermonic Meditations on the Book of Ecclesiastes.* Eugene, OR: Wipf and Stock, 2006.

GAJ   *The Gospel according to Judas.* Colorado Springs: Helmers and Howard, 1991 (revised edition Colorado Springs: Navpress, 1994). The classic work on betrayal, forgiveness, and grace.

HTRG   *Historical Transcendence and the Reality of God.* Grand Rapids: Eerdmans, 1975. The seminal work formulating Anderson's incarnational theology in relation to the transcendence of God.

Abbreviations

JAJ — *Judas and Jesus: Amazing Grace for the Wounded Soul.* Eugene, OR: Cascade, 2005. A follow-up to *The Gospel according to Judas.*

LSBL — *Living the Spiritually Balanced Life: Acquiring the Virtues You Admire.* Grand Rapids: Baker, 1998. On the virtues and the Christian life.

MGB — *Minding God's Business.* Grand Rapids: Eerdmans, 1986 (revised edition, Eugene, OR: Wipf and Stock, 2008). A theology of leadership in Christian organizations.

MOTF — *Ministry on the Fireline: A Practical Theology for an Empowered Church.* Downers Grove, IL: InterVarsity, 1993. Anderson's theology of mission.

NAS — *The New Age of Soul: Spiritual Wisdom for a New Millennium.* Eugene, OR: Wipf and Stock, 2000. A response to New Age spirituality.

OBF — *On Being Family: A Social Theology of the Family* (with Dennis B. Guernsey). Grand Rapids: Eerdmans, 1985. Explores the implications of *On Being Human* for family life and ministry.

OBH — *On Being Human: Essays in Theological Anthropology.* Grand Rapids: Eerdmans, 1982. The seminal book on Anderson's distinctive theological anthropology with wide implications for ministry.

SOG — *The Soul of God: A Theological Memoir.* Eugene, OR: Wipf & Stock, 2004. A virtual "greatest hits" of Anderson's theological ideas in the context of his life and ministry.

SOH — *The Seasons of Hope: Empowering Faith through the Practice of Hope.* Eugene, OR: Wipf & Stock, 2008. Provocative thoughts on the theological significance of the seasons of life seen in light of hope.

SC — *Self-Care: A Theology of Personal Empowerment and Spiritual Healing.* Wheaton, IL: Bridgepoint, 1995. A theology of the emotions, with attention to abuse, shame, betrayal, tragedy, and grief, building upon the theological anthropology in *On Being Human.*

SCSS — *Spiritual Caregiving as Secular Sacrament: A Practical Theology for Professional Caregivers.* New York: Jessica Kinsley, 2003. A unique proposal for acknowledging the spirituality yet not necessarily religiosity in all caregiving.

SOM — *The Soul of Ministry: Forming Leaders for God's People.* Louisville: Westminster John Knox, 1997. The mature statement of Anderson's theology of ministry.

Abbreviations

SOSN   *Something Old, Something New: Marriage and Family Ministry in a Postmodern Culture.* Eugene, OR: Wipf & Stock, 2007. A follow-up to *On Being Family* addressing contemporary concerns and issues.

SPT   *The Shape of Practical Theology: Empowering Ministry with Theological Praxis.* Downers Grove, IL: InterVarsity, 2001. Various classic essays on the theology of ministry.

SP   *Soulprints: Personal Reflections on Faith, Hope, and Love.* Huntington Beach, CA: Ray S. Anderson, 1996. Anderson's existentially powerful journal as a young pastor.

TDD   *Theology, Death and Dying.* Oxford: Basil Blackwell, 1986. Builds upon Anderson's suggestive ideas on a theology of death and dying in the context of ministry in *On Being Human*.

TFM   *Theological Foundations for Ministry.* Edited by Ray S. Anderson. Grand Rapids: Eerdmans, 1979. A massive anthology that is a theological education in itself including generous amounts of Barth, Bonhoeffer, and the Torrances as well as Anderson, especially the classic essay "A Theology for Ministry."

UW   *Unspoken Wisdom: Truths My Father Taught Me.* Minneapolis: Augsburg, 1995. Lessons on the development of character based on relationships between parents.

I. ON THEOLOGY AS MINISTRY

1

"EXPLORATION INTO GOD"

The Doctrine of God and God's Ministry

Ray Anderson suggests that whenever we write the name of God on the chalkboard (or PowerPoint!) we should then step back and see if we survive! To speak of God is an awesome thing. Too often glib theologians and confident ministers may too easily speak of the divine. Should this lead us to agnosticism, or at least a halting skepticism about any knowledge of God? What, instead, if we began to speak of God in terms of *ministry*?

But is this right? If we ever speak of the ministry, of the church, the sacraments, etc. then should that not be based on thoroughgoing and convincing arguments for the existence of God and explicit knowledge of God's nature? Ray Anderson has an alternative.

All Ministry is God's Ministry

To speak of the ministry of God means to speak of the God who acts. Every Bible-believing Christian adheres to this. But so often we interpret ministry as only *our* part, which we do after God has acted. Isn't it more biblical to speak of ministry as something that, in the first instance, *God* does? "All ministry is first of all God's ministry."[1]

---

1. *SOM*, 5.

God acts in creation and then in Israel. These acts are the ministry of God. The general ministry of God in creation becomes particular and specific in the election of Israel. "Revelation is not just the Word of God to Abraham; it *is* Abraham."[2] Abraham is not just the object of revelation, he is now a part of the ministry of God. What distinguishes the God of Israel from the false gods is that the God of Abraham is the creator who acts (Ps 135:18), the one who possesses a ministry. The God of Abraham is the God who acts, who has a ministry.

In that same seminal essay, "A Theology for Ministry," Anderson speaks of ministry as both "revelation and reconciliation."[3] Building upon Karl Barth's and T. F. Torrance's critique of Cartesian and Kantian influences on modern theology, Anderson argues for regarding revelation and reconciliation as "reciprocal movements of a single event."[4]

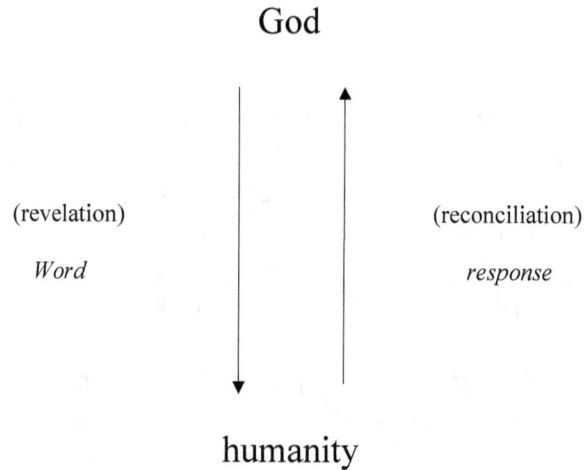

FIGURE 1

God is on "both sides" of revelation and reconciliation—not just knowing God through revelation (the attention of the Cartesian and Kantian agendas), but through the ministry of reconciliation as well. That God is on the side of reconciliation as well as revelation will be important for Anderson when he appropriates T. F. Torrance's doctrine of the vicarious

2. "A Theology for Ministry" in *TFM*, 19. A later form of this essay is found in "A Practical Theology of Ministry," in *SPT*, 61–74.

3. *TFM*, 9–12.

4. *TFM*, 11.

humanity, not just the death, of Christ.⁵ Yet Anderson is careful to make it clear that reconciliation is not a movement that originates with the fall of humankind, but that which is integral to the endowment of the *imago Dei*, the image of God in humanity (Gen 1:26–27). "The human response does not condition or determine the divine Word, for the Word has itself a divine correspondence by virtue of the image of God through which Adam knows himself."⁶

Yet there is a ministry of "judgment and grace" to the solitary male Adam, in the first "not good" of the Bible (prior to the fall in Gen 3): "It is not good that the man should be alone" (Gen 2:18).⁷ God does the ministry of that which is impossible. "It is only when the single male is put to sleep and the creative Word itself operates in such a way that the divine likeness and endowment is divided into a complementary existence, that that possibility is actualized. Out of impossibility, God's Word becomes God's ministry."⁸ Adam now exclaims, "This at last is bone of my bones and flesh of my flesh" when Eve is created (Gen 2:23). Both judgment and grace are found here, Anderson argues. "This grace of God is a verdict rendered upon every attempt to circumvent that Word and to provide an alternative response. It is revelation that provides reconciliation. God's ministry takes what is impossible and creates possibility."⁹ But in doing so, Anderson hastens to maintain the place of human participation. "But it does this in such a way that the creature himself is incorporated into the new possibility. It is 'bone of my bone and flesh of my flesh.' Adam is not himself set aside. There is no judgment against him, but a judgment for him and against all that would only inevitably betray and fail him."¹⁰

---

5. See T. F. Torrance, *Mediation of Christ*, 73–98; Anderson, "The Practical Theology of Thomas F. Torrance" (available on-line at http://www.tftorrance.org). A crucial aspect of understanding the vicarious humanity of Christ is that "Jesus did not come to introduce his own ministry. His ministry was to do the will of the Father and to live by every Word that proceeds out of the mouth of God . . . Christ's primary ministry is to the Father for the sake of the world, not to the world for the sake of the Father. This means that the world does not set the agenda for ministry, but the Father, who loves the world and seeks its good, sets the agenda." *TFM*, 7–8.

6. *TFM*, 11.
7. *SOM*, 57.
8. *TFM*, 14.
9. *TFM*, 14.
10. *TFM*, 14.

Our understanding of the *nature* of God, our *doctrine* of God should be shaped by God's ministry, Anderson contends. Where else, apart from God's activity in Israel and in Christ, do we get our doctrine of God? The greatest possible being we can think of? A great designer? A source of morality? No! From the story of God-at-work in Israel and in Christ.

Anderson finds the meaning of God's ministry in the seventh day (the Sabbath), the "special word of revelation from God."[11] Through the Sabbath, the meaning of the first six days are revealed. "In this way, one can say, theologically, that the seventh day precedes the sixth day. In the same way, God's ministry precedes our concepts of God. It is through God's ministry of redemption that we understand the meaning of God's work as Creator."[12] Without the Sabbath, the seventh day, we are left with only the six days, the days of nature, the days of the workaday world in which nature determines destiny, in which our jobs, for example, can determine wholly who we are.[13] A concept of a God of nature or destiny can unfortunately be brought into the church. It is different when the seventh day theologically precedes the first six days, Anderson suggests. Therefore, our concepts of God are judged, a God of our morality or our culture, something that makes us very uncomfortable.

God's ministry reaches its fruition in Jesus Christ, the perfect manifestation of ministry as revelation and reconciliation in the one event of the incarnation of God. Jesus is the act of God who is the lord of the Sabbath; the one who can say, "The Sabbath was made for humankind, and not humankind for the Sabbath" (Mark 2:27).[14] Allowing the disciples to go counter to the religious authorities and instead meet human need on the Sabbath, Jesus is saying something about the nature of God. Religious authority does not triumph over human need.

The church's doctrine of God has implications for its ministry. The church is obviously involved in ministry. But whose ministry is it? Do we realize that every act of ministry we perform says something about our doctrine of God? Unfortunately, our actions often reveal very poor doctrines of God, Anderson contends. Why do we exclude children from the communion table? Doesn't that say something about who God is to us—a

---

11. *SOM*, 4; *TFM*, 16.
12. *SOM*, 3.
13. *TFM*, 16.
14. *SOM*, 8.

God who demands a certain age in order to commune with him; a God who really does not love children until they can recite certain doctrines?[15] Or does our attitude towards divorce reveal a God who really puts stipulations on his love, whose forgiveness and reconciliation is indeed limited? "Every act of ministry reveals something of God."[16] This includes the theological task: "God's ministry is the revelation of God to humans and the basis for all human knowledge of God's nature and purpose. There is no theological task that has any basis in God's truth other than the task of expounding the ministry of God."[17] Theologians and pastors, take note!

A God of Presence, Not of "Omnis"

Ray Anderson is fond of speaking of an incident early in his pastoral ministry: After unleashing a barrage of sermons on the doctrine of God with the classic attributes of omnipotence, omniscience, and omnipresence, a parishioner came over to Ray and asked (I'm paraphrasing), "All these things may be true. Does it make any difference that God can do anything, if he cannot do *something*, something in my life?"[18]

It may be easy to discount the parishioner's exasperation as just another example of a person shaped by our "me-centered" society, with an anthropocentric theology that defines God in terms of what God is for us. That is indeed a perennial theological problem. If we speak of Christ for us, *Christus pro nobis,* are we not tempted to define God only in terms of "Christ and his benefits" (Melanchthon)? Nevertheless, it is better for God to be somewhere than everywhere, Ray Anderson has said. For the sake of the ministry of God, the doctrine of God needs to be conformed to that ministry. The ministry of God is the ministry of the God who acts, not the God we just talk about. He is the God of the Exodus, of Moses and the burning bush, who reveals his name and purpose to Moses, the first "theologian" in the Bible.[19] Moses is the first theologian because he tells even the Genesis story from the perspective of the exodus from Egypt. He knows for himself the act of God; that it is better for God to be some-

---

15. *SOM*, 7
16. *SOM*, 8.
17. *SOM*, 6
18. *SOG*, 20.
19. *SOM*, 3.

where than everywhere. The genuine doctrine of God, who God really is, is found in such a ministry.

Ultimately, ministry is for the sake of those whom God loves. The Christian gospel lives or falls with the self-revelation of God in Jesus Christ: "All things have been handed over to me by Father, and no one knows the Son except the Father, and no one knows the Father except the Son and anyone to whom the Son chooses to reveal him" (Matt 11:27). Scripture functions here as a testimony to this self-revealing God, not as a corpse that is the object of dissection, dissecting truths out of a dead body.[20] No, the God of Jesus Christ, whilst he remains inconceivable and incomprehensible, lives because Jesus lives. "What if one assumed that the life, death, and resurrection of Jesus is the very self-revelation of God's own being?"[21]

At this point, Anderson is ready for what he calls, with some adventure, "exploration into God": "Do I dare set aside my theological books and launch out into an exploration into the soul of God revealed only through Jesus?"[22]

What Does It Mean to Explore into God?

Taking the term from a poem by Christopher Fry, Anderson speaks often of the theological project as "exploration into God."[23] For him that means both a very personal exploration (in contrast to the pseudo-objective academic theologian!) that is very ministry-oriented, and therefore, human-need-oriented and church-oriented. He is constrained to do this by his Christology: "Jesus is literally the exegesis of the soul of God," finding the soul, or center, of theology in the soul, or center, of God.[24] Thus, the heart of ministry is an incarnational theology, based on Jesus' prayer to the Father: "As you have sent me into the world, so I have sent them into the world" (John 17:18). Anderson explains its power in reinvigorating his own ministry when he was a pastor at the church in Covina: "The soul of theology is found in the *as*, while the soul of ministry is discovered

20. *SOG*, 21.
21. *SOG*, 22.
22. *SOG*, 22.
23. *SOG*, 23.
24. *SOG*, 23.

in the *so*. I seized upon the *as* and the *so* as the hinge on which God's self-revelation through Jesus turns toward the world for the sake of its reconciliation to God."[25] Exploration into God has begun.

Love Is the Logic of God

The love of God is the first step of exploration into God for Ray Anderson. Anderson was struck by a famous lecture by Edward J. Carnell, then president of Fuller Theological Seminary, in which Carnell argued that it was love, not truth, that most characterized a theological seminary.[26] In a day in which evangelical theology had rallied around the defense of truth in a secular age as the distinctive of Christian apologetics, Carnell found himself roundly denounced by many.[27]

"It is far easier to say one believes in God than to say that one is loved by God."[28] Believing that one is loved by God in a world of untold innocent suffering can sometimes be a mighty task. The logic of God is not to be found in analytical truth but in the Son lying at the bosom of the Father from all eternity (John 1:18). This is what it means for Jesus to be the *Logos*, the Word of God. He is not a bare-bones principle of "Reason" or order. "What is irrational, is to tear reason and logic out of the heart of love and to define the truth of God in impersonal doctrinal formulas which issue from and are under the control of a human logos."[29] Those who accused Carnell of being irrational and subjective, Anderson contends, were the ones guilty of irrationality and unreasonableness.

Love as the logic of God immediately brings us to our knees in confessing our inadequacy.[30] "To say too little about the love of God may be worse than attempting to say too much. On the other hand, it may be the case that to take of but a portion of divine love is to grasp the whole."[31]

---

25. *SOG*, 24.
26. *SOG*, 75.
27. Marsden, *Reforming Fundamentalism*, 147ff.
28. *SOG*, 77.
29. *SOG*, 77.
30. *SOG*, 78.
31. *SOG*, 78.

READING RAY S. ANDERSON

The Passionate, Yet Not Promiscuous, Love of God

God's love is a passionate love. Many popular theologies, such as Rick Warren's *The Purpose-Driven Life*, are so fond of leaping to anthropomorphisms about God that one wonders if the nineteenth century philosopher Ludwig Feuerbach's familiar criticism that religion is just the projection of our highest values is really behind such talk. Can Anderson avoid such criticisms?

"The love of God is passionate but not promiscuous," Anderson claims.[32] Disinterested love is supposed to be a virtue of God's unconditional *agape* love, but is it really? Disinterest is an indication of a failing relationship. Anderson has often counseled a married person to make a date with their spouse. Promiscuity does not allow for any commitment in its acts of love. That is why animals do mate but do not meet.[33] "In the case of God, love is a verb before it can be a noun. We discover that God is love only because God acts in loving ways."[34] His love is passionate yet not promiscuous. "We should not shrink from expressing God's love in terms that reflect the passion of God by which he enters into the human situation so fully that it requires him to enter the depths of human estrangement."[35]

God enters into human estrangement. The "exploration into God" then will not be without human disorder, tragedy, suffering, and sin. The God revealed by the "exegesis" of Jesus will not permit anything less.

Since God enters into human estrangement, we must not fear anthropomorphic language about God. The Bible, and our human personhood, demands it: "How can I give you up, Ephraim? How can I hand you over, O Israel? . . . My heart recoils within me; my compassion grows warm and tender" (Hos 11:8). "The love of God for the people who became unlovely is itself lovely."[36] Anderson is rather indignant at how many theologians have emasculated the doctrine of God: "When the poet and the prophet speak of this passionate love that God is, how dare our theologians turn

---

32. *SOG*, 78.
33. *OBH*, 53.
34. *SOG*, 79.
35. *SOG*, 79.
36. *SOG*, 79.

"Exploration into God"

back from the promised land of love to the barren desert to stare at the bush which never burns."[37]

What does it mean to speak of a God who enters into human estrangement? Will that not threaten the doctrine of the God who is immutable (unchanging) and impassible (not forced by another)? That is of secondary concern for Anderson. What is at stake is a theology that reflects God's risk in entering into human estrangement, an actual theology in ministry with hurting people. "Knowing the passion of love in our own hearts, even when it leads us astray, we ought to know better than to worship a God who has never felt the hurt of lost love or the joy of embracing a found child."[38] This does not mean, however, that God is so wedded to the creation that he loses his freedom, as is the temptation for process theology or open theism.[39] As passionate but not promiscuous, "divine love does not go out searching for just anyone to love, it reaches out to love everyone with love."[40] There is a subtlety here that may be difficult to grasp. Again, Anderson sees divine love as very particular, yet not exclusive as in "tulip" Calvinism.[41] Yet the freedom of God is still there: "If divine love is troubled, it is not by anxiety or unrest within love itself. What arouses passion in the love of God is not an unfulfilled need, but a longing to

---

37. *SOG*, 80.

38. *SOG*, 80.

39. Process theology, based on the philosophy of Alfred North Whitehead, argues for a God whose love means a serious dependency upon the world. See John B. Cobb, Jr. and David Ray Griffin, *Process Theology: An Introductory Exposition*. Open theism reflects the same concern but does not venture as far as process theologians, only suggesting that God is "open" for some of the future to be changed, for example, by intercessory prayer. See Clark Pinnock, et al., *The Openness of God*. Anderson is sympathetic to a degree with the Open theists and the element of "randomness" that God has placed in the world, yet he would emphasize "a more Christological analysis of God's relation to the world where God's power is grounded in God's love for the world expressed through the incarnation, death and resurrection of Jesus." *DWW*, 108–9

40. *SOG*, 80.

41. The "tulip" in "tulip" Calvinism refers to the doctrines reflected in the Synod of Dort (1618–19) (Total depravity, Unconditional election, Limited atonement, Irresistible grace, and the Perseverance of the saints), which are thought by some to have been a logical development of the thought of John Calvin (1509–64). The teachings of Dort developed in its English-speaking expression mainly through the Westminster Confession and Catechisms. See James B. Torrance, "Strengths and Weaknesses of the Westminster Theology" and T. F. Torrance, "The Westminster Tradition," in *Scottish Theology*, 125–55, especially 141.

embrace the divine image in another."[42] At this point Anderson is deep into the doctrine of the Trinity, but a doctrine of the Trinity that involves the triune God actively and profoundly in ministry with estranged humanity, not just a "badge of orthodoxy" to be recited and then forgotten the next day. "The life of the Father does not belong to the Father alone, but also to the Son, and those who become partakers of that life."[43]

"The Silent Tears of Unborn Sin"

"The Silent Tears of Unborn Sin" is a title of a sermon once preached by Ray Anderson, whose content he cannot remember but whose title speaks of suffering deep within the soul of God.[44] (Maybe some titles are better than their sermons!) What remains poignant for Anderson is the truth of the King James translation of Rev 13:8: Jesus is "the lamb slain from the foundation of the world." "How far back into the soul of God, I wondered, could we trace the love which led Jesus to the cross to die the death resulting from the sin of Adam and Eve?"[45] If Jesus cries, then God cries. Anderson stretches our imaginations to consider whether or not our ministries reflect these tears. Maybe there should be more tears in ministry (apart from bad sermons)! "The tears shed by Jesus at the tomb of Lazarus and over the city of Jerusalem were the tears of God as surely as Jesus is God."[46] God has wept from all eternity over our tragic planet and twisted lives.

Is There a Tragic Place for Love in God?

Does God, however, do nothing but cry with us? one might ask Anderson. For Anderson, love is not sentimentality but the hard encounter of two; God and humanity, or Adam and Eve. Therefore, there will be a jostling for space, a potential for disagreement, or at least misunderstanding. Love will be a place, a context, where the encounter is stretched. Perhaps Anderson would be well served to develop his theology of the ontological

---

42. *SOG*, 80.
43. *SOG*, 81.
44. *SOG*, 82.
45. *SOG*, 82.
46. *SOG*, 82.

as a place in God that involves risk, and even negotiation, but at least a vital eternity of life between the Father and the Son in the Spirit. Certainly Anderson's supralapsarian emphasis on "the lamb that was slain from the foundation of the world" echoes this (that grace precedes the Fall). For Anderson, because love creates this space, there is no power to compel or coerce the other.[47]

This place of love is a place that is one with the tragic. Anderson tells of the great opposition he hears from students when he speaks of the tragic in God. "For some strange reason they feel more comfortable with the idea that all human 'dis-ease' comes from sin. They see no virtue or good in the tragic. They want divine love, at least, to be a deep flowing stream with no rocks or rapids."[48] The problem is that they cannot accept the tragic "as a reality of love."[49]

We have come full circle, back to the incarnation, which proclaims that in Jesus Christ we do not know the reality of love except as the reality of the tragic. This is not Reinhold Niebuhr's category of the ontological tragic but a christological reality. Ralph Wood is right to criticize Niebuhr for elevating the tragic to a theological principle.[50] Barth is preferable, Wood argues, because the gospel does not leave us weeping but in the victory of the resurrection of Christ. Anderson admits with Niebuhr that the tragic and the ambiguous are reflected in human experience, but he does not stop there. For Anderson, the tragic is found as christological and issues forth from the church in ministry, confronting a tragic world and making decisions in ministry that are not innocent and righteous at times but with ambiguity in their midst. I remember Anderson frequently speaking of the need for "a doctrine of ambiguity" in the church. Like Batman in the film, *The Dark Knight,* he is a hero but not the hero Gotham City wants—unambiguously clean.[51] Was this not the problem that Jesus' contemporaries had with him? Is the church most of all concerned with protecting its reputation, a tragedy that Dietrich Bonhoeffer all too personally experienced in the church in Germany in the 1930s and 40s? We are back to Anderson's incarnational theology and ministry, a theology

---

47. *SOG*, 84.
48. *SOG*, 84.
49. *SOG*, 84.
50. Wood, *The Comedy of Redemption.*
51. *The Dark Knight,* directed by Christopher Nolan, Warner Bros. Pictures, 2008.

and ministry that does not try to protect its innocence but risks all because of its incarnational love. "The passion of love with its capacity to embrace the tragic is the enduring power of faith. I suffer for those who dare not love for fear of having to let go, in time at least, of that which is loved."[52] Anderson dares to say that God does that. "Embracing the tragic element imbedded in the act of love at the beginning is not to be afflicted with sadness but to have faith in love."[53] That is the kind of love that God is.

"God comes to us in the reality of our frustration and does not force us to deny that which is real to affirm that which is merely true."[54] Our desperation for God is often found in demanding that God be found anywhere but in our suffering. "Those who in desperation claim 'spiritual' victory over emotional needs may be simply experiencing psychological repression supported by theological concepts. Behold we are sterilized! Spiritually aseptic, capable of neither pain nor desire! If this is faith (and God) then we will oblige. Call us unspiritual if you must, but leave us the dignity of at least being lost!"[55]

God is not afraid of our suffering. It is we who, because of our nervous doubt, desperately try to defend God. That is why attempts at a theodicy are so weak pastorally. Anderson likes to say that the purpose of ministry is not to be an apologist for God but to stand on the side of humanity, even against God! Many will not follow Anderson at this point, but the challenge to the church is then, How can we say that our ministry participates in the same ministry of Jesus? "If there are two sides to humanity . . . Christ will be found on the wrong side."[56] God can defend himself. So also the minister cannot "answer" the terribleness of grief: "No substitute is worthy to replace the grief for what has died."[57] It cannot be explained (for it is a miracle), but there is a miracle of redemptive suffering:

> But left to make the tragic hour a part of our life, suffering weaves the rent sadly into the fabric of faith. From deep within ourselves comes feeling greater than emotion to direct emotion into redemptive grief; a deeper grief than unrequited love to transform love into wisdom, and wisdom into joy. We may never laugh again without a

52. *SOG*, 85.
53. *SOG*, 85.
54. *SOG*, 51.
55. *SOG*, 51.
56. *SOG*, 73; cf. *HTRG*, 252.
57. *SOG*, 51.

tear, but we will love again. And not with love that moves with desperate anxiety, with compulsive need, but love enriched by suffering. Love that leaves the other free to love, knowing that only such love is worthy of the name, only such love a sufficient relationship.[58]

Love is free and not coercive (in contrast to abusive relationships) because God is both free and not coercive.

The Inner Life of God Is Made Outer

What are we then saying about God? Anderson certainly builds upon Karl Barth's insistence that Christology is essential to our doctrine of God. The "double movement" of the incarnation, from God to humanity and then from humanity to God, is not to be restricted to a sequential order.[59] While there might be some truth that the first movement is the movement of God coming into solidarity with humanity and the second movement is that of Christ's substitutionary atonement in the entirety of his life on our behalf, the double movement involves simultaneously an act of God and an act of humanity, in the deity and humanity of Jesus Christ. There is no "doctrine of God" that does not include our humanity. While this may seem to be stressing the "economic" Trinity (who God reveals himself to us in his revelation) at the expense of the "immanent" Trinity (who God is eternally in himself), the intention is to ground our "exploration into God" in God's self-revelation into the depths of our humanity. The pastoral implications of this are profound. The minister is not the mediator between God and humanity. Only Jesus Christ is (1 Tim 1:5). Reconciliation should no longer be viewed as only subsequent and dependent on revelation.[60] There is one act of God in Jesus Christ and it includes both revelation and reconciliation, the humanward movement and the Godward movement. "This does not mean that the truth of revelation depends upon our own subjective apprehension of it. Rather, our subjective self is brought within the sheer objectivity of God's self-knowledge."[61] How often does the church argue about the fineries of its doctrine of revelation and leave reconciliation unspoken and not lived in our world?

58. *SOG*, 51–52.
59. *SOG*, 71.
60. *SOG*, 71.
61. *SOG*, 71.

READING RAY S. ANDERSON

The reality of reconciliation wedded to revelation is the response of Jesus Christ on our behalf, what Anderson's mentor Thomas Torrance has called, "the vicarious humanity of Christ."[62] "Jesus is also the response which humans make to the Word of God. Thus, revelation is complete in Christ, both as to its source in God and its response from the human side."[63] Anderson can even be this strong: "It would not be wrong to say that Jesus is the true believer, whose own faith in the Father becomes the basis for our faith in such a way that we are freed from the ambivalence and inward uncertainty which always plague our own attempts to believe. It would not be wrong to say that Jesus is also the true disciple, whose own obedience lived out in the face of temptation in such a way that we are freed from our own instability and unreliability of will."[64] In other words, exploration into God is integrally connected with the humanity of Christ because God does not choose to reveal himself apart from our plight, misery, and needs. "Practical theology" is not a luxury or addendum to the theologian's curriculum.

All of this leads us irretrievably to the doctrine of the Trinity. The Trinity, therefore, is not based on *a priori* romantic versions of community or abstract speculation but on the concrete life and ministry of Jesus. "In this way both revelation and reconciliation take place through our being in Christ being in us. In the account of Jesus' life and ministry while he was on earth, the inner life of God has opened up to us a life of selfless love."[65]

The inner life of God, however, is not to be discovered apart from the discovery of the self. The incarnation of God in Jesus Christ will allow nothing less. Since God became human, Dietrich Bonhoeffer said, we can no longer speak of God apart from humanity or humanity apart from God.[66] This is not to make God "manageable" to our needs or perspectives but to take seriously the radical nature of Immanuel, God with us (Matt 1:23). Citing Jer 29:13, "When you search for me you will find me; if you

---

62. *SOG*, 72; See T. F. Torrance, *The Mediation of Christ*, especially 83–98, "The Mediation of Christ in our Human Response." Cf. the importance of the vicarious humanity of Christ that Anderson finds in Torrance's practical theology in Anderson's last published work, "The Practical Theology of Thomas F. Torrance," (available on-line at http://www.tftorrance.org).

63. *SOG*, 72.

64. *SOG*, 72.

65. *SOG*, 72.

66. Bonhoeffer, *Ethics*, 82.

seek me with all your heart," Anderson comments, the inner life of God is not to be known without an outer expression. That is the ministry of the church, the continuing ministry of Jesus Christ.

The being of God reveals an inner life that always confronts an Other. That is the meaning of the doctrine of the Trinity for ministry, not just speculation or correct doctrine. "There is the reality of 'another,' a thou to whom my being responds as 'I.'"[67] The Trinity has prepared us for such an encounter. That is why the doctrine of God, or rather, our "exploration into God," is always *particular without being individualistic*: "I do not love everyone, nor am I loved by everyone. Yet, I do look for the 'thou' in others and so strive to 'love my neighbor as myself.'"[68] The God of Anderson's "exploration into God" is a down-to-earth, grassroots God who is not afraid to be involved in our mess and who owns up to his own mess! He is the God of Jesus Christ. Anderson then can be so frank as to say, "I do not strive for the uniqueness of being God, but I no longer distinguish between His reality and my own."[69]

"I can no longer distinguish between His reality and my own." Blasphemous? Anderson, the maverick that he is, is not afraid of the charge. But what he means is that he is not going to defend an abstraction apart from the flesh of Jesus Christ, the flesh that encountered men and women in the trenches of life. There really was a "downward" or "humanward" movement in the incarnation. And that says everything about God (that we can say). I can no longer abuse others for the sake of doctrinal purity, ecclesiastical power, or denominational polity. I am too close to them because God is too close to us. The lines of distinguishing are blurred so that we share the same apartment. *De jure*, by law, there is a distinguishing between God and humanity. *De facto*, by the facts of where and how we live, we have no such luxury; God has no such luxury. This is "exploration into God," but not God without humanity, not without the soul of God.

What Does God Want? What Does God Do?

Sigmund Freud is famous for saying, with probably a smirk and sarcasm, "What do women want?" He probably did not stay for an answer. Ray

---

67. *SOG*, 53.
68. *SOG*, 54.
69. *SOG*, 54.

Anderson may ask, "What does God want?" because he is simultaneously enthralled with "exploration into God" and challenged by that exploration amidst the tragic of this world.

How do we discern God's will? Is everything caused by God? "Something, rather than everything." Anderson liked to say this a lot and it is certainly true when applied to the power of God. Again, he is not about to limit the power of God to world processes or the finitude of our minds. Yet, since "exploration into God" is a christological venture, when we ask questions of God's will and God's providence, we are constrained by the double movement of the incarnation of God in Jesus Christ. The "historical transcendence" of God as found in the incarnation is restricted to the historical reality of Jesus of Nazareth, but it is a transcendence nonetheless. Jesus is the transcendence of God, not an "omni-cause." When Anderson was confronted by a woman who had been told that God had caused the death of her child, he responded, "I could no longer defend this doctrine. She was pressing toward the soul of God and I followed her. I told her that the death of her child was not predetermined by God, was not known by God in advance, and was not caused by God."[70] Does he go too far at this point? Is there not great security in believing that "the whole world is in his hands"? Anderson has said that the place of ministry is not to defend God but even to take up the laments of others against God. If God is all powerful and we are faced with unspeakable horror, do not the laments of Jesus Christ, even from the cross ("My God, my God, why have you forsaken me?") give us not only the right but also the imperative to *stand against God*, because we know, through Christ, that he is all powerful and all good? Yet when Jesus Christ becomes an integral part of our doctrine of God, and a critique of the traditional doctrines of immutability and impassibility, we can see why Anderson would dare to "explore into God" even at this point.

God Is on Both Sides

Much of the preceding thinking about the doctrine of God in Ray Anderson's thought saw its germination in his doctoral dissertation, published as *Historical Transcendence and the Reality of God*. Using the contemporary crisis in theology of speaking of the transcendence of God

---

70. SOG, 175.

in an increasingly secular age, Anderson develops a thoroughgoing christocentric doctrine of God, so that he can speak of both transcendence and immanence because Jesus Christ is both God and human. God is on both sides. If Jesus Christ is the Word of God, we do not have the permission to speak of another or preliminary God behind the back of Jesus. Therefore, the doctrine of God is from the beginning intrinsically connected with the ministry of Jesus.

The transcendence of God is a pastoral as well as an epistemological problem. "The problem is not: what kind of assertion are we making when we say 'God exists as the Wholly Other,' but rather: how can we make any assertion *at all* about a reality that is 'wholly other'?"[71] Where is God in the middle of the night of one's personal tragedy? Fundamental to Anderson is that for him, like Barth and Torrance, the Being of God is known in his Act: "The act-character of God's being . . . constitutes for us a 'hermeneutical horizon' beyond which we cannot go, but which is a *real* horizon because its rationality is not conferred upon it by the world with which God intersects, but by the God who acts."[72] The incarnation is *the* act of God, but not to the exclusion of the risen Christ acting in the church through the Spirit in concrete acts of love. This act is communal because, in Bonhoeffer's words, "Christ exists as community."[73] There is no Word of God apart from a Work of God.[74] Again, God is on both sides. Revelation is not done half by God and then completed by our response.

Historical transcendence frees one up to consider God as acting in the mundane and ordinary of life. This is true for Anderson in how he richly draws upon his South Dakota farm experience and particularly the quiet wisdom of his father.[75] The attraction of Bonhoeffer's "religionless Christianity" is not in some exaltation of secularism but in bridging the gap between the supernatural and the natural.[76] That is what the historical transcendence of the incarnation does for us in terms of the doctrine of God.

---

71. *HTRG*, 39.
72. *HTRG*, 70.
73. Bonhoeffer, *Sanctorum Communio*, 141, 189ff., 199ff.
74. *ETEC*, 117–37.
75. *UW*.
76. *HTRG*, 94.

READING RAY S. ANDERSON

The Church Is Christ in the World

Anderson is critical of those who use Bonhoeffer's "religionless Christianity" as a way to *find* Christ in the world.[77] Rather, the church is to *be* Christ in the world. This was demonstrated graphically in Bonhoeffer's own life as Anderson poignantly writes: "The circle of historical transcendence was closed by Bonhoeffer in a way that was entirely consistent with his theology and his life. His final, normative, ontic relationship was with the hangman, who slipped the noose around his neck. This was normative, not merely for Bonhoeffer, but for the world. It was the ultimately non-religious word which had been incarnated as the penultimate. The world was being transcended again by the 'suffering God'—the circle is closed."[78]

Thus for Anderson, as much as for any Roman Catholic or Eastern Orthodox theologian, ecclesiology is closely connected with the doctrine of God and not left to a much later consideration, as is the case for most Protestants. The particularity of the incarnation demands this. Yet can Anderson avoid the Protestant criticism of Roman Catholic and Eastern Orthodox theologies of equating Christ with the church and so very easily identifying every action of the church with that of Christ? To borrow a category from T. F. Torrance, is there a *contingent* relationship between Christ and the church so that even though we do wish to speak of an *organic* relationship between Christ and the church, Christ remains the "head" of the "body"? The Pauline literature in the New Testament, of course, speaks many times of Christ as the head over all things, including, the church (1 Cor 11:3; Eph 1:22; 4:15; 5:23; Col 1:18; 2:10, 19). By contingence Torrance means "that as created out of nothing the universe has no self-subsistence and no ultimate stability of its own, but that it is nevertheless endowed with an authentic reality and integrity of its own which must be respected."[79] Torrance admits the difficulty of the idea because "the independence given by God to the creation is itself dependent upon God."[80] Both creation and incarnation contribute to our understanding of contingence: creation coming "out of nothing," dependent yet having been given a certain autonomy by God, and incarnation reminding us

77. *HTRG*, 95–98.
78. *HTRG*, 98.
79. T. F. Torrance, *Divine and Contingent Order*, vii.
80. T. F. Torrance, *The Trinitarian Faith*, 100.

"Exploration into God"

of our desperate need to be reunited to God.[81] The church is organicially connected to Christ but should never try to set its own agenda apart from Christ the head. Again, for Anderson, God is on both sides because of the incarnation, providing a constant christological critique of the temptation of the church to set its own agenda while maintaining its ontological connection to Christ. This christocentric ecclesiology that profoundly affects the doctrine of God will be developed much more in part two, "Ministry as Theology," chapters 4 through 6.

God Here and Now

God Here and Now is a collection of sermons by Karl Barth.[82] This is a good way to speak of one of Anderson's concerns. His "exploration into God" is a reality in the present, full of flesh and blood because the incarnation was full of flesh and blood. "More uncanny than the *mysterium tremendum*, which lurks in the grotesque shapelessslessness of the startled imagination, is the event-full intimacy of a familiar face. More disturbing than the unknown intentions of a stranger, are the knowing footsteps of an approaching friend. More awe-full than a disembodied spirit, is the flesh of an incarnate God."[83]

Notice how seamlessly Anderson weaves together the amazing encounter with the human face and that with the flesh of the incarnate God, yet, unlike in many theologies, the distinction is still there. God is here and now, in the presence of the other. Building upon T. F. Torrance's scientific theology, one can be free to be confronted by reality; of God, the person, and the world: "For what really happens, is not that we grasp the truth through the sheer power of intellect, organizing bits and pieces into a whole, but we are grasped in our whole person by the inescapable reality of truth as it confronts us."[84] God here and now. And humanity here and now.

Still, the "here and now" is always particular for Anderson. Thus Israel is not just one of the species of revelation but the creation of an unique divine act, just like the incarnation: "This self-communication

---

81. T. F. Torrance, *The Trinitarian Faith*, 101.
82. Barth, *God Here and Now*.
83. HTRG, 103.
84. HTRG, 105.

of God through what we may call a Name-act, marked Israel off from all others, but also served to place the reality of God *in* the world even as he was marked off *from* the world. Thus, Israel could only know its God by starting from the concrete act, not from the universal idea of the godhead."[85] Again, the particular and the concrete is the stuff of theology, and therefore, all genuine theology is practical and personal theology. Once I heard the well-known Orthodox theologian David Bentley Hart say with a smirk before a large crowd, "I haven't a pastoral bone in my body." He has said that in print in an interview as well.[86] For him, this seemed to be a point of academic pride. For Anderson, it would be a point of shame. Shame, because the incarnation, the historical transcendence of the living God is particular and concrete, providing a critique of many of our traditional abstract and impersonal doctrines of God. "God's transcendence must be seen *as* his humanity, not merely *in* his humanity."[87]

A Case Study to Consider:
"Where Is God When Evil Strikes?"[88]

Facts and Dilemma

Sophia (not her real name) is from a small town in the Midwest and attends a Christian high school in a nearby city. Her senior year has finally arrived; it should be a year full of memories, activities, excitement, and anticipation. However, for Sophia, this school seems to be a continuation of the struggles she has endured for the past three and a half years. During the last two weeks of her junior year she finally confided to a teacher that her father had been abusing her for more than three years. Sophia's willingness to seek help, share with her mother what had been happening, and report the abuse to the proper authorities was the result of almost a school year's worth of developing a relationship of basic trust with the teacher she confided in and prayer from two other teachers who had been observing Sophia's bizarre behavior during the school day.

---

85. HTRG, 112.

86. David Bentley Hart, "Where Was God? An Interview with David Bentley Hart," 28.

87. HTRG, 118, n. 32.

88. This case was provided by Marcia Dillon, a graduate student in ministry at Friends University.

"Exploration into God"

Sophia's mother was called to the school and Sophia shared with her what had been happening between herself and her father. Fortunately, her mother was very supportive. The legal authorities also were notified and following the graduation of one brother and the junior high promotion of another, the father was ordered to leave the home. As a result of the actions taken by Sophia, her two younger brothers have a sense of relief that he is gone. Sophia's older brother and other members of their extended family, however, are extremely upset with her for making such "outrageous" accusations. In fact they have accused her of lying and trying to destroy their family.

As well as trying to deal with the disruption of her family life, anger from her siblings, grandparents, and some aunts and uncles, Sophia has severe issues with God and his apparent disregard for her heartfelt prayers at the beginning of the abuse. She prayed for the abuse to stop, questioned why her father behaved in such a despicable way, and asked why she had been targeted for the treatment she was receiving. It did not seem that God was there when she asked to be delivered from the abuse as it occurred.

Questions to Ponder

1. Ray Anderson says, "Every act of ministry reveals something of God." What would you say to Sophia that reflects "God's ministry" to Sophia even now as a reflection of who God truly is?

2. Remember that the "omnipotence" of God has largely become a problem for Sophia. But what is the "something" that God may do even now in Sophia's life?

3. What difference would Jesus Christ make for Sophia's vision of God, given what she has gone through? (Anderson: "What if one assumed that the life, death, and resurrection of Jesus is the very self-revelation of God's own being?") How can Jesus be "the exegesis of the soul of God" for Sophia?

4. "It is far easier to say one believes in God than to say that one is loved by God." Can Jesus be understood as the *Logos* of a God of love for Sophia despite the irrationality and absurdity of this world? Where does Sophia find the love of God then?

5. How does God in Christ embrace human estrangement and tragedy, such as Sophia's? How would this be different than other concepts of God (consider the doctrines of immutability and impassibility)? Is there a danger in making God too anthropomorphic?

6. "The passion of love with its capacity to embrace the tragic is the enduring power of faith." How can Sophia view God differently if God embraces the tragic?

7. Is it helpful to stand with Sophia in accusation against God? Is this christological? Can this actually be a ministry of God, even of the vicarious humanity of Christ?

8. How is the Trinity the basis for accepting the reality of Sophia's tragic situation? See also Anderson's statement, "I do not strive for the uniqueness of being God, but I no longer distinguish between His reality and my own." Does Anderson bring God into Sophia's life or confuse God with Sophia's problems?

9. How does the church relate to who God is to Sophia? How is this reflected differently in Sophia's relationships: (a) with the teacher and (b) with her relatives? What is the significance of John 17:18: "As you have sent me into the world, so I have sent them into the world" in ministry to Sophia?

2

ON BEING HUMAN

Theological Anthropology and the Humanity of God

Being Encountered by the Person Before Us: The Foundation of Practical Theology

God has become human. Ray Anderson's theology of incarnation gives birth to an incarnational ministry. This means that the human must never be sacrificed for the sake of defending the reputation of God. God does not need that, as we see in the very act of the incarnation. Thus theological anthropology is not simply a droll discussion of soul, spirit, and body or what the image of God consists of in human beings. Theological anthropology is an issue of ministry; critical issues that demand that we encounter and respect human beings as they concretely exist, in joy and despair. "A theological anthropology has no starting point but human existence itself, within this world of time and chance."[1] But Anderson follows Karl Barth in his critique of "non-theological anthropology," either mythical or philosophical.[2] Both arise from what the human being can understand of oneself.[3] In addition, sin mars our perspective on ourselves. As Barth

1. *OBH*, 15.
2. *OBH*, 8–15.
3. *OBH*, 12.

comments, "For what we recognize to be human nature is nothing other than the disgrace which covers his nature; his inhumanity, perversion and corruption."[4]

Anderson's pastoral theology will not forfeit the human for the sake of theological orthodoxy. This becomes a genuine challenge to evangelical theology. "The problem of a non-theological anthropology, it turns out, is not that the human person is the starting point, but that the human person seeks to have the final word, the decisive judgment, as to the nature of humanity."[5] In contrast to non-theological anthropologies, we are not left abandoned but are embraced by a Word that comes from outside humanity but not external to humanity because of the incarnation; a Word not only of God but also about what it means to be human. This stands, however, as a critique of our attempts at self-salvation. What stands before us is the actuality of the human person, not just one's potentiality. This is expressed in both the doctrines of election and covenant, doctrines usually ignored in discussions of theological anthropology.[6] In election, we see that the actuality of the human person that God creates comes before the possibility of the ideal human person.[7] "We can become human because we are in fact divinely determined to be human and *are* human."[8] Existentialism does the opposite, beginning with a possibility that will hopefully lead to an actuality. The particularity of election begins with the election of Jesus Christ (following Karl Barth), "the firstborn among many brethren" (Rom 8:29), so that election becomes something of inclusion not exclusion, election as "the affirmation of the self."[9] So also covenant is seen as "the relatedness of the self," belonging in the midst of our brokenness.[10] Anderson is fond of quoting the scientist and philosopher Michael Polanyi, "Our believing is conditioned at its source by our belonging."[11] "Personal individuality is not an original given fact; it is achieved through the differentiation of the self within the structure of

---

4. Barth, *Church Dogmatics*, III/2, 27. Cf. *OBH*, 15.
5. *OBH*, 16.
6. *OBH*, 162–72.
7. *OBH*, 165.
8. *OBH*, 165.
9. *OBH*, 162.
10. *OBH*, 169.
11. Polanyi, *Personal Knowledge*, 322 and *OBH*, 169.

relation."[12] To be human is not just to be in existential *angst* but to be in relationship. "The point we are making is that each person is ontologically rooted in personal being in such a way that belonging is more fundamental and determinative of our being than existential estrangement or confusion."[13] The critical question that may be posed to Anderson is, How does one then minister to a person in estrangement, particularly in loneliness? The answer for Anderson would not be simply to exalt solitude but to acknowledge a "presence in absence" (to borrow from the Orthodox theologian John Zizioulas), the eschatological word that lives by faith not by sight (2 Cor 5:7).[14] So we must love but we always love being aware that "there is something inherently tragic about the form of our present community of human love. No person is ever totally 'at hand' to us. Even if it should appear to be so in any given moment, there is an inevitability of separation and distance which each person must traverse."[15] Giving people a bromide of false community or the bliss of solitary existence can be dehumanizing. Humanity as co-humanity, as important as it is, can also be cold comfort.

The Reality of Crucified Humanity

Theological anthropology is often plagued with defending the ideal. The ideal family and the ideal human being (seen as religious) are presented as the goal for ministry. But is that what the ministry of Jesus Christ is all about?

Crucified humanity involves humanity as God finds it. Thus, judgment is not foreign to Anderson's theology, in contrast to much of modern and postmodern theology. This is because we first know the grace of God: "It is precisely by starting with humanity as it comes under the most radical judgment of God and as it experiences the most radical grace of God that the original form of the human is revealed to us."[16] The barrenness of Sarah is just as important as Abraham's faith.[17] This is still a profoundly

12. *OBH*, 169–70.
13. *OBH*, 171.
14. Zizioulas, "Human Capacity and Human Incapacity," 420. In Zizioulas, *Communion and Otherness*, 206–49, 420. Cf. *OBH*, 177.
15. *OBH*, 177–78.
16. *OBH*, 16.
17. "The Grace of God Which Presupposes Barrenness." In *SOM*, 43–51.

christological starting point for it is in the cross of Jesus Christ that we know crucified humanity: "It is then to the humanity of Jesus Christ, the one crucified and judged for all humanity, who bore in his own humanity the radical judgment of God, that we turn as the starting point for theological anthropology."[18] Anderson is suggesting something very difficult yet profound for theology: maintaining a christocentric anthropology while holding to the importance of the particular and concrete human person that we encounter. At this point, a pastoral, practical theology merges with the kind of christocentric theology that Karl Barth advocates. A theology of historical transcendence joins together with a theological anthropology: The transcendent God is near to us in Jesus Christ, near to our very particular, concrete humanity. This has tremendous pastoral implications. Anderson is fond of describing the pastoral counseling situation as dependent upon keeping eye contact. The moment the counselor loses eye contact they have lost the one being counseled. This is a christological as well as anthropological issue. For in Jesus Christ, "the radical form of the original is present; he reveals the true form of humanity not as one who in his innocence kept a distance from our humanity but as one who took on himself our own humanity."[19]

Knowledge of crucified humanity is not possible for non-theological anthropologies.[20] For the reality of what it means to be truly human is revealed by Jesus Christ in his faith and obedience that leads to the cross (Phil 2:5–11). Non-theological anthropology only knows humanity in its disorder. In Christ there is the true order of being human, yet he is also the one who "emptied himself, taking the form of a slave, being born in human likeness . . ." (Phil 2:7). He reveals what the true form of humanity is as he simultaneously judges our humanity on the cross. Non-theological anthropologies are not able to do that. "They cannot infer the true order of humanity from humanity under judgment. One cannot infer a healthy being from a sick one. One cannot reconstruct order from disorder. The absence of sickness is not yet health."[21]

"The absence of sickness is not yet health." Anderson is saying something very profound here about grace and sin. Our tendency is to present

18. *OBH*, 16.
19. *OBH*, 16.
20. *OBH*, 17.
21. *OBH*, 17.

grace as the cure for sickness. But do we really know what health is? Do we really know what it truly means to be human? The Christian revelation is not only the revelation of God but also the revelation of what it means to be human. Grace is needed to reveal the true order of humanity. Otherwise, the "cure," in the case of much of religious excess, can end up destroying humanity. The sad history of religion, including Christianity, is a powerful testimony to that. The critique of religion by Karl Barth and Dietrich Bonhoeffer was aimed at exposing the insidiousness of its force and destructiveness towards humanity. The man born blind was not the victim of his parents' sin or his own sin, Jesus proclaims (John 9:2–3). "There is no direct equation between human creatureliness and sin. But this is only revealed to us through the humanity of Jesus himself."[22] In contrast, the cross destroys the principle of sin by its grace: "The deterministic principle of sin is broken, and grace is revealed as the true order of humanity.... The point here is that a theological anthropology dares to begin with humanity because it can find in the humanity of Jesus Christ the true order of humanity and the true nature of sin as the source of disorder and destructiveness."[23]

Furthermore, crucified humanity does not end with the cross but the resurrection of Jesus Christ.[24] The western, Latin tradition is so indebted to the "law—sin—grace" *ordo salutis* (order of salvation) that we forget Paul's words that Jesus "was raised for our justification."[25] "The continuity between Jesus of Nazareth as the crucified one and Christ the Lord as the resurrected one is the indispensable foundation for a theological anthropology."[26] Otherwise, we have forgiveness but no new life. "What the cross and death appear to have cancelled out, the resurrection restores and affirms. Jesus' resurrection authenticates humanity as creaturely humanity under the determination of the Word and power of God, fully able to live within the conditions of a temporal and earthly existence but not finally subject to the determination of a creaturely nature."[27]

22. *OBH*, 17.
23. *OBH*, 17.
24. *OBH*, 18.
25. James B. Torrance, "The Unconditional Freeness of Grace," 11–12; Anderson, "Did Jesus Have to Die on a Cross?" in *DWW*, 69–78; "When I Survey the Wondrous Cross" and "I Serve a Risen Savior" in *SOG*, 107–25.
26. *OBH*, 18.
27. *OBH*, 18.

READING RAY S. ANDERSON

Discovering the Creaturely in Humanity

In our rush to discover what the image of God in humanity is, we often neglect the very important biblical teaching that we are also creaturely. Yes, we are made in the image of God (Gen 1) but we are also made of the dust (Gen 2). Anderson, desiring to meet the concrete, particular, actual human person in a pastoral situation that participates in the continuing ministry of Jesus Christ, wrestles honestly with the implications of humanity as creaturely.[28]

Anderson presents this axiom: "Creatureliness is an undifferentiated field upon which the occasion of the human occurs."[29] By this Anderson means that we cannot avoid the fact that to become human is to share the same creatureliness with the rest of God's creatures. We are all creatures of the sixth day of creation. The difference will be in humanity's participation and recognition of the seventh day, the day of rest, the last day.[30] Even as a boy on the farm, Anderson shares, preparing the animals for slaughter, there was "some sort of psychical transference" when the day of slaughter arrives; the animals cowered in the corner, knowing the day had come. "The momentary demonstration of fear expressed in this intimate and yet terrible event of death may have showed a glimmering of the solidarity of the sixth day."[31]

Any qualitative distinction between the human and our fellow creatures cannot be accepted. There is a relationship, however, that does not determine all that it means to be human. The human being is not just the physical. There is, however, a *contingent* or non-necessary connection between humanity and creatureliness.[32]

The determination of the human is not to be found in an Aristotelian *telos,* a purpose that is fulfilled when possibility moves into actuality but is an eschatological reality determined by the Word of God.[33] That is the meaning of the last day, the seventh day of creation. "The seventh day is contingent on a determination from beyond or outside the continuum of

---

28. *OBH,* "Humanity as Creatureliness," 20–32.
29. *OBH,* 21.
30. *OBH,* 22–23.
31. *OBH,* 23.
32. *OBH,* 24.
33. *OBH,* 24.

the first through the sixth days."[34] The human being as creature, therefore, has not an intrinsic *telos* which is not just "natural law." "Creatureliness itself cannot determine the human."[35] This has tremendous implications for facing physical or mental deformities in a pastoral situation, and particularly for practices of abortion or euthanasia. Yet the state of the biological is not irrelevant to human personhood. May it not be more merciful to terminate the life of a baby born without a brain than to preserve the life no matter what? Still, the image of Governor Sarah Palin, once nominated as the Republican vice-presidential candidate, holding her newborn Down's Syndrome baby, having chosen to bring the child to term, reminds many of how our culture often, in contrast, marginalizes, if not discards, those who are not physically or mentally perfect.

To be human is not to be limited to the accessible and empirical. This is something that only a theological anthropology can say, but it must say it. Otherwise, our value for the human is only limited to that which we can perceive.[36] Yet, this is still a part of the actual knowledge of the human, the human as determined not just by nature but by the Word of God. "If creatureliness has no immanent teleology which determines the human, we must attribute the *telos* of humanity to some source other than the creaturely condition under which it exists."[37] Creaturely nature is therefore relativized: "To a great extent our creaturely being will certainly determine how far we realize our human potential. Genetic defects at conception or pathological conditions of gestation and birth may cause a human being to enter life grotesquely disfigured and deformed. Yet, because creaturely being is insufficient as a determinator of human being, it is also powerless to deprive a human being of that which is distinctively human."[38] The caution is sounded here that we must not despise the creatureliness of ourselves and others. "For there is no person other than the one who meets us as a creaturely being."[39]

---

34. *OBH*, 24.
35. *OBH*, 25.
36. *OBH*, 27.
37. *OBH*, 28.
38. *OBH*, 28.
39. *OBH*, 29.

READING RAY S. ANDERSON

The Problem of a Criterion for the Human

Creaturely nature is relativized and, therefore, perhaps is our understanding of "health." "It would appear that human beings are both more vulnerable at the creaturely level and yet have more tolerance for creaturely disorder."[40] If the human being is more than the creature, then the health of the human being should be defined by something beyond only its important, yet relativized, creaturely needs.

> Can order be inferred out of disorder? Can health be inferred out of sickness? If all empirical study of human personhood must begin at the creaturely level and with some degree of disorder, by what criteria can we establish the true order of the human as a goal for life, or as an objective in therapy? If something is to be inferred out of disorder, it may only be that the nature of the disorder is such that it points to an order of human existence which lies beyond creaturely possibilities.[41]

What is it in natural, creaturely behavior that will determine that which is unnatural?[42] Again, Anderson points to the humanity of Christ, the "original form" of what it means to be human. In Christ's humanity there is a liberation from the determinism of our creatureliness. Our creatureliness does not determine who we are. "Here we can avoid the deterministic error of equating physical or psychical dysfunction with sin, and yet deal with sin radically and thus redemptively without fear of destroying or offending that which is truly human."[43]

Thus, one can be a very eccentric and perhaps psychologically suspect Old Testament prophet and still be healthy. This does not mean that creaturely health, both physically and psychologically, is unimportant. It is only relativized. "It would be intolerable to think that God is less concerned for the creaturely aspect of our existence than for the human, for under his determination they are experienced as a unity of being. However, because of the contingent relation between the human and the creaturely, one cannot produce a human person by perfecting the creature, nor can one destroy the human (in the sense of invalidating what God has

---

40. *OBH*, 29.
41. *OBH*, 29.
42. *OBH*, 30.
43. *OBH*, 30.

given) by afflicting the creature."⁴⁴ This has tremendous implications for pastoral care. Is the goal simply a morally and spiritually perfect human being? Is that who is represented by Anderson's attention to the humanity of Christ? That may be the danger, if it is not maintained by Anderson that Christ's humanity is vicarious, it represents us and takes our place, and is not simply an ideal that cruelly exhorts us. Anderson realizes the danger of the tyranny of perfectionism: "If one is informed by a theological anthropology in seeking to help others, one is freed from the tyranny of perfectionism and the obsessions about physical and psychological concerns which it produces."⁴⁵ Anderson sees that determinism is at the heart of perfectionism: "Perfectionism is essentially bondage to a deterministic principle, whether the principle is grounded in natural or supernatural causes. Perfectionism holds out the carrot of 'security because of good health' or 'favor with God' at the end of a stick labeled 'correct behavior' or 'conformity to the right rules.'"⁴⁶ While not mentioning the vicarious humanity of Christ at this point, Anderson sees that the distinction in the humanity of Christ is liberation, not simply making one good: "Theologically speaking, it is more important to be a liberated person than a 'healthy' or 'good' person, if liberation is understood as human creatureliness set free to realize its destiny in God, while goodness or health is merely the perfection of the creaturely for its own sake."⁴⁷ Determinism and perfectionism are always temptations for one's anthropology (both Augustine and John Wesley; Calvinism and Arminianism).

Anderson's refusal to limit the human to the ideal is particularly relevant to medical ethics. In fact, speaking of "human being as a marginal possibility," he argues that the creaturely is a contingent aspect of humanity, and therefore, not only should it be included as the "field" on which the human occurs, but also the creaturely does not determine that which is human. "Not everything which comes from the body of a human person is human—but some things are," particularly mentioning the remains of a miscarriage as an agonizing problem.⁴⁸ "It is the task of a theological anthropology, however, to know the difference between what

---

44. *OBH*, 31.
45. *OBH*, 31.
46. *OBH*, 31–32.
47. *OBH*, 32.
48. *OBH*, 148–50.

is coincidental and what is identical, for only by being able to posit the contingent relation between humanity and creatureliness can we hold in check the fatalistic determinism of creaturely nature itself, so that the human person is free to have his or her own destiny beyond the possibility of creaturely nature."[49] However, Anderson quickly adds, "it does not follow that it is ever within our power of determination to say that a malformed infant, no matter how deformed or deprived of what we consider normal human capacity, is less than human."[50] The key is the problem of "what we consider" to be human. Here Anderson will follow the importance of the concrete, particular encounter of what is human, not an abstract or ideal. As Anderson in another place distinguishes between "discrimination" and "free will," he will argue that human autonomy, particularly if another human being is involved, is not a final criterion for theological ethics: "To esteem 'freedom of choice' as an expression of individual autonomy and the basis of human dignity and responsibility is to miss the point. The so-called freedom to be the 'master of my fate, the captain of my soul' is at bottom joyless and cheerless. For this is a freedom which denies dependence on the other as the source of one's own personhood."[51]

Again, Anderson pleads for beginning with the actual, particular human being, what he refers to as the "middle zone" that does not make moral decisions based on the beginnings or endings of human life.[52] A pastor may baptize a stillborn baby but not an embryo in a petri dish.[53] "Some things are just not right because they offend our sense of decency. This is middle zone morality."[54] Does this open Anderson to charges of simply arbitrary choice? Do we really have the wisdom to know or do we too easily delude ourselves with rationalizations out of convenience's sake? Anderson responds, "Those who differ might argue that this is a very subjective way of thinking and creates the so-called 'slippery slope' by which anything could be allowed. My response is that nothing is more objective than the actuality of human being and human life. And that if, we begin with the middle zone, we are beginning with objective real-

---

49. *OBH*, 148.
50. *OBH*, 150.
51. *OBH*, 82.
52. Anderson, "When Does Human Life Begin?" in *DWW*, 111–22.
53. *DWW*, 115.
54. *DWW*, 117.

ity, not merely subjective theory."[55] This means that there is a place of responsibility, in an openness to being led by God in an intervention, like the one mentioned by Anderson, the microcephalic and neurologically damaged fetus or the teenager hopelessly upheld only by the "god" of technology, the ventilator.[56] Here is when ethics becomes contextualized into a responsible act by the community of faith, "the community of God as custodian and steward of the mystery of life," daring not just to protect its innocence but practicing a ministry of intercession that includes yet goes beyond prayer.[57] "It is one thing to have outlined the reality of being human under the various aspects of the theological curriculum; it is quite another to become human through the labyrinth of errors that confront us without and within."[58] This is being encountered by the concrete person. This is the objectivity of God becoming human in Jesus Christ and its profound implications. In this encounter we can see humanity as determined by the word of God.

Humanity as Determined by the Word of God

Our creatureliness cannot bear the burden of explaining our humanity in totality. So much of all artistic and scientific achievement stills cries out for completion; alienation still exists in the most accomplished of artists. What God *says* is something quite different; a word from outside that is the true determination ("And God said to them . . ." Gen 1:28). There is no potential in human beings that can create this word. It has come from outside. The way is being prepared by Anderson for a theological anthropology that is determined by the other; a quite distinctive trinitarian anthropology. The doctrine of *creatio ex nihilo* (creation out of nothing) provides the foundation for the creative Word. "Theologically, the doctrine of creation *ex nihilo* protects creation from both determinism and perfectionism."[59] The determination of creation comes from outside, yet the distinction between creator and creature is always maintained.

---

55. *DWW*, 119.
56. *DWW*, 119–22.
57. *OBH*, 153–58.
58. *OBH*, 158. Cf. the entire chapter, "Being Human—In Fear and Trembling," 146–58.
59. *OBH*, 35.

The soul, spirit or some distinction has often been declared to be that which is distinctive in the human being, the *imago Dei*, the image of God (Gen 1:27). Anderson argues with much of contemporary scholarship that "soul" or "spirit" are not separate entities but that which opens the human being toward God. "What is distinctive about human beings is not that they have a 'soul,' which animals do not possess, but as 'besouled body' and 'embodied soul,' the 'spirit' of that existence is opened toward God in a unique way as the source of life. The whole of human life, body and soul, is thus oriented toward a destiny beyond mortal or natural life."[60] However, this is not to destroy the concept of the soul into mere physical reductionism. "Without some understanding of the soul, we cannot fathom the depths of our depravity, the delirium of our obsessions, nor the delights of our imaginations. Nor can we clarify and conform our most profound spiritual aspirations, without a sense of the soul."[61]

In an age that champions equality and equal rights above almost everything else, it is hard to speak of *differentiation* as an essential part of being human, as Anderson does. As he boldly states, "That which we call human being is differentiated creatureliness, experienced as response to the creative divine Word."[62] Differentiation is not based on observations deduced from natural law, but God's being as Trinity, that God is differentiated within himself. "Even as God exists as differentiated from his creation, he also exists as a differentiated being. According to the Christian doctrine of the Trinity, God exists as three in one. As Father, God is differentiated from the Son, and both Father and Son are differentiated from God as Spirit. This is revealed through the incarnation, which shows God to be 'on both sides' of the relation between himself and his people."[63]

Years before the rash of interest among contemporary theologians in the doctrine of the Trinity, Anderson saw great implications of God's triune being for theological anthropology. Yet, much of the contemporary emphasis is rightly on the *perichoresis*, the mutual indwelling, or relationships within the three persons, persons-in-communion. Anderson suggests that differentiation is just as important as the identification, particularly for theological anthropology. So the "response-ability" of

60. Anderson, "Theological Anthropology," 85. Cf. Anderson, "On Being Human," 75–94.
61. Anderson, *NAS*, 13.
62. *OBH*, 35.
63. *OBH*, 36.

humanity to respond to the divine Word is not a latent capacity within the human or the result of a deterministic sovereign decree, but grounded in the differentiation within God himself, particularly in the eternal Son's response to the Father in the Spirit. This is also the intra-trinitarian foundation for the vicarious humanity of Christ. Anderson makes this plain in *Historical Transcendence and the Reality of God*: "I would say that the transcendence of *inter*-actions is the image of the transcendence of *intra*-action."[64] So even Anderson's emphasis upon co-humanity should not be seen as an abstract principle divorced from the ontological relationship between the triune God and humanity as made in the image of the triune God. Anderson adds, "This is why I have said that the ontic structure of community is not in co-humanity, not even in a co-suffering-humanity, but rather, it is in the intra-divine transcendence concretely given in the Incarnation."[65] The implications here are suggestive, particularly for the question of gender identity. In Genesis 2, Adam lacks this differentiation. "In order to be completely human, one must experience differentiation as the content of one's own life. In naming the animals, there was apparently no 'response.'"[66] The creation of Eve changes this. "God then puts Adam to sleep and 'differentiates' his state of singleness by creating two where there was only one."[67] This differentiation was created by the Word of God. God creates the response. "This response is experienced not only as that of a single being but as co-humanity."[68] The result will be a theological foundation for both awareness and freedom.[69] Anderson will run further with Barth's idea of "co-humanity," perhaps more than any other contemporary theologian.

Humanity as Essentially Co-humanity

Of what does "co-humanity" consist? For Anderson, this is no less than "the radical structure of humanity itself."[70] This will not be to the oblit-

---

64. *HTRG*, 181.
65. *HTRG*, 184.
66. *OBH*, 36–37.
67. *OBH*, 37.
68. *OBH*, 37.
69. *OBH*, 37–43.
70. *OBH*, 44.

eration or ignoring of the individual. Yet, because of "a certain radical priority . . . given to the 'we'" . . . one must say that "there is no way in which the 'I' can be self-determined for determination is fundamentally an act of differentiation."[71] From here we can enter into that which seems very similar, although Anderson does not make this explicit, to the self-giving *perichoresis*, or mutual indwelling between the Father, the Son, and the Holy Spirit in the Trinity: "An individual person must first of all be differentiated as person in contrast to the world of impersonal being. This can only take place in a reciprocal act by which the other recognizes and affirms the singularity of one's own particular existence."[72]

Co-humanity, however, should not be considered apart from creatureliness, as Anderson advocates so strongly. Therefore, the dualism between the spiritual and the physical, the religious and the social is cut across decisively, not based on a "worldview" but on a structure of being human. In a diagram Anderson picturizes in co-humanity two individuals in relation, with a "double movement" within each (reminiscent of the "double movement" of the incarnation of both revelation and reconciliation that is the foundation for Anderson's theology of ministry), brought together by the "social-self."[73]

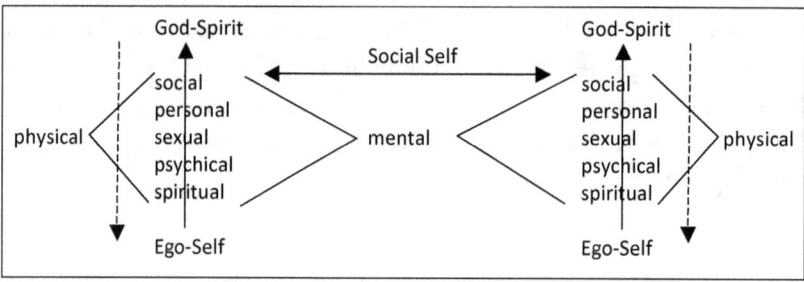

FIGURE 2: from *Spiritual Caregiving*, 40

Co-humanity, therefore, begins with the development of the social, not the spiritual self, as Christians often think. God respects the creaturely, including parenting. Leading on (the dotted lines) through the development of the personal, sexual, psychical, one then comes to the spiritual, from which the second, solid lines go back toward God. Without this

71. *OBH*, 45–46.
72. *OBH*, 46.
73. *SOSN*, 28. Cf. *SC*, 31 and *SCSS*, 40.

"double movement," the physical and mental sides "will become either rationalistic or mystical—both essentially movements away from the concreteness and embodiedness of the self."[74] Again, Anderson returns to the absolute importance of the concrete, embodied, particular human person versus an abstract, rationalistic or mystical (religious) self.

Co-humanity as Male and Female

The great biblical case study for co-humanity is Genesis chapter 2. This is a main theological reason why gender must be granted a unique perspective in differentiation. "We are two before we become one," Anderson can say.[75] This is not determined by nature, as most ethics grounded in gender differentiation argue, but on grace.[76] God interrupts Adam's solitary existence with the creation of Eve. "Nature" has not fulfilled Adam's need for differentiation. "There is a differentiation of creatureliness itself which is constitutive of the human, not merely differentiation between the human and the non-human, or even differentiation between the human and God. . . . Thus the woman emerges as the counterpart to the man out of the act of differentiation, not merely as another instance of differentiation."[77] Differentiation by gender, therefore, is not arbitrary. This reciprocity of being is not created by any possibility in Adam; it is an act of God.[78]

Freedom of being, therefore, is not the act of the individual Prometheus, asserting himself or herself but comes out of a reciprocity of being: "Only when the human is experienced as reciprocity of being as an immediate and spontaneous recognition is the freedom of being made manifest."[79] Again, allusions can be made to the mutual self-giving within the Trinity. Yet out of this relationship, the particular singularity of Adam (and Eve) arises. "That is, one is not a singular person as part of a social structure of human being without also being particularly male or female."[80] In contrast to Martin Buber, the I and the Thou includes

---

74. SOSN, 29.
75. OBH, 46.
76. OBH, 47.
77. OBH, 48.
78. OBH, 48–49.
79. OBH, 49.
80 OBH, 50.

sexual identity and therefore does not ignore humanity in its particularity. Marriage and family, also, is not burdened with being a first order of humanity, but being male or female is. "One does not have to be a brother or sister, husband or wife, in order to be human. But one does, according to our understanding of co-humanity, have to be either male or female."[81] Marriage and family is therefore relativized for the single person, who is often regarded as "incomplete" by church tradition yet the monastic idea of celibacy is not to be seen as the ideal for the Christian.[82] Anderson is one of the few theologians whose theological anthropology has a ringing significance for the single person and can still emphasize the communal nature of being human.

Creatureliness returns as the undifferentiated field on which the human occurs.[83] This includes gender but with a distinction; for Anderson, following Karl Barth, male and female in the human becomes the occasion for the image of God in humanity (Gen 1:27).[84] For human beings, sexuality is not just for "mating" but also for "meeting": "In a certain sense, animals participate in sexual distinctiveness only as a part of their creaturely nature; we speak of animals 'mating' but not 'meeting,' in the sense of the meeting of persons in which differentiation produces singularity of being."[85] Yet Anderson is careful to add that "male and female is not a 'boundary concept' dependent on precise definitions or descriptions, but it is an order of existence which makes boundary decisions meaningful, though these decisions must always be made in the face of certain ambiguities."[86] Tragedies and accidents in nature exist (e.g., hermaphrodites) but grace, not nature, should determine our theology. This essential polarity also becomes a critique of social structures that seek to apply culturally accrued roles of being male or female to an "order of creation."

The true order comes from God. The otherness to which being male or female points is ultimately that which is found between God and creation. "The differentiation between Creator and creatures is not a barrier to relation. Indeed, that which is totally 'other' *constitutes* the basis for

---

81. *OBH*, 52.
82. *OBH*, 52.
83. *OBH*, 21.
84. *OBH*, 51–52.
85. *OBH*, 53.
86. *OBH*, 54.

relation of persons and is the source of true intimacy. Intimacy is intensified by otherness."[87] Instead of an argument for same sex relationships, the "other" or the "different" is not just to be found in social relationships, but one might even add, ultimately, in God himself as Trinity. The "other" is more ontologically connected with Father, Son, and Holy Spirit, and then secondarily with the distinction between the Creator and creation, and then finally in the order in humanity as male and female. The "sameness" of homosexual relationships manifests a disorder. "We can put the ontological question this way: did the divine Word that summoned me into being as a human person—and therefore determined that I would be either male or female at the level of creaturely being—also determine an essential polarity for me? Is there an intrinsic order to sexual identity?"[88]

What is crucial in the debate on homosexuality is not simply the interpretation of a few isolated biblical texts but the question of whether or not theological anthropology will speak to the entire human being. "If gender identity and the polarity of male and female are acquired and accidental aspects of our personhood, we should leave sexuality to the psychologist and the ethicist, and go on about the business of a theological anthropology."[89] Not all human disorder is caused by sin; some are just tragic. So the homosexual may have such attractions that go against God's order. "If one takes Genesis 1:26–27 as the foundational text for understanding human sexuality as rooted in the divine image, then sexual orientation may be considered a personal and biological differentiation expressed through the 'ordered ontology' of male and female, male or female."[90] This is God's "preference," that we dare to say because we believe in divine revelation, grace, not just our perceptions of nature.[91] But the incarnation of God in Jesus Christ begins with God's "presence." "If one holds that God's preference for human sexual relationships follows the created order of male and female rather than same-sex co-habitation, this does not rule out God's gracious presence in the lives of those who find it impossible to live by the divinely created preference."[92] Practically

---

87. *OBH*, 105.

88. *OBH*, 110. Cf. "Homosexuality: Theological and Pastoral Considerations" in *SPT*, 266–83.

89. *OBH*, 110.

90. *SOSN*, 142–43.

91. *SOSN*, 143.

92. *SOSN*, 143.

speaking, this means a church that is willing to participate in the unconditional grace of the presence of Jesus Christ while simultaneously bearing witness of God's order for human beings in maleness and femaleness. "The church as the body of Jesus Christ expresses both divine preference and divine presence in the lives of its members."[93] In a way, Anderson may be saying that this is a manifestation of the "double movement" of the incarnation that he speaks of in his theology of ministry, both humanward, in revelation, and Godward, in reconciliation. The humanward movement is that of presence and solidarity; the Godward, of precedence and *theosis*, being conformed to the image of his Son (Rom 8:29). The church often errs when it emphasizes solidarity at the expense of *theosis* or *theosis* at the expense of solidarity, just as justification without sanctification or sanctification without justification.

Anderson's other discussions on the contingent nature of our creatureliness may provide a response to the other assumption, that I am determined by what I perceive my "orientation" to be. Anderson refuses a theological anthropology that depends upon nature and our perceptions of nature, but instead on a unity of nature and grace predicated on the epistemological priority of the grace revealed in Jesus Christ. The *imago Dei* is revealed to us as concretely manifest in our sexual polarity. The implications of this are profound. "Thus, 'he' and 'she' belong to the same theological dogma as *imago Dei*. To fail to be able to relate 'he' and 'she' as specific instances of created humanity to the *imago Dei* is to cut the *imago* out of this historical and creaturely level of human personhood, with the result that the empirical self is surrendered to the social scientist while the theologian can only attempt to describe the ideal self."[94] This has far reaching implications for the whole interface between theological anthropology and ethics, an interface that is often sadly lacking, reflecting the widespread dichotomy between theology and ethics.[95] "For this reason some theologians resort to ethics when dealing with matters pertaining to human sexuality. But such 'theological ethics,' not properly grounded in theological anthropology has recourse only to abstract values such as 'human good,' or 'liberation,' or 'social justice' in deciding particular instances of human behavior."[96] At stake is whether or not sexuality is under

---

93. *SOSN*, 143.
94. *OBH*, 111.
95. See Stanley Hauerwas, "On Doctrine and Ethics," 21–40.
96. *OBH*, 111.

the divine Word. "However, if sexuality is indeed an intrinsic polarity of being expressed as gender identity, then we can identify the true order of human sexuality as an order of being human itself."[97] Therefore, gender identity is not accidental to personhood but essential.[98]

If gender identity is both ontological and an eschatological goal of the self, then stereotypes of masculinity and femininity should not be permitted.[99] This is not to say that differentiation between the male and the female should be unrecognized. Complementarity of being is an essential lesson of the creation of Eve in Genesis 2. As the *imago Dei*, gender identity reflects the complementarity in God's own being as the Trinity. "God reveals himself through the incarnation as a reciprocity of being-in-relation, expressed as Father, Son, and Holy Spirit," so that "the Father ordains, and the Son subordains his own will to that of the Father."[100] Related to his teaching on "historical transcendence," Anderson does not view the self-emptying of the Son as the obedience of an inferior to a superior, or "an emptying of sovereignty, but a manifestation of the sovereign God in his activity of reconciling the world to himself."[101]

Anderson is speaking here of what he calls "the hierarchical modality," in analogy to the relationship between the Father and the Son, because sexuality (along with all of human creatureliness) is not tangential but essential to humanity. Yet like creatureliness, gender identity does not sum up all that is human, or all that is the *imago Dei*. "Essential sexuality, as that fundamental polity of being which differentiates us as persons, may then be said to exist coincidentally with but not identically to creaturely sexuality. We cannot equate the differentiation of the *imago Dei* with creaturely sexuality as absolutely identical, any more than we can equate the *imago Dei* as absolutely identical with creaturely being, for that would mean that everything that had creaturely being would also be the *imago Dei*."[102] In other words, one must be careful not to avoid the eschatological dimension of sexual polarity. "The command of God which summons the human creature into existence and which determines the order of existence is not identical with creaturely origins or even a creaturely order of

97. *OBH*, 110.
98. *OBH*, 110.
99. *OBH*, 112–13.
100. *OBH*, 114.
101. *OBH*, 115.
102. *OBH*, 117.

existence."¹⁰³ In other words, one does not begin with natural law, but with grace. "On the other hand, precisely because these temporal orders are eschatologically relativized, they cannot be determinative for personhood nor for existence as co-humanity in its ultimate intentionality. To live as husband or wife, mother or father, is to live responsibly under the command of God, but the sociological role order itself cannot be determinative of the command of God."¹⁰⁴ Lying behind this is Anderson's concern for particularity in human personhood. The concrete human person, who is either male or female, is the person who stands before us, who is our neighbor, not any abstract conception of humanity (or sexuality!).

Discrimination as an Alternative to Free Will

Existentialism can make much of the virtue of free will; as does the Arminian and Semi-Pelagian traditions in the church, from Methodism to Eastern Orthodoxy. Anderson is not happy with making a choice (no pun intended) between grace and faith or determinism and free will. It is a pastoral issue for Anderson, for at the heart of the theological question of grace vs. free will, or how they relate to one another, is the practical question of the Christian, "What is the will of God?"

Human beings are addressed by the divine Word and therefore human subjectivity cannot be ignored. "We do not first of all know ourselves, and then search for a divine, transcendent Word to know and grasp. We are first of all grasped and known; then follows knowledge of ourselves."¹⁰⁵ Knowledge by the other means that a response is demanded. Indecision is not a human response but that of the "double-minded" person, unstable in all of one's ways (Jas 1:8). "In this sense healthy, vigorous subjectivity is a result of a good relationship, not the cause of it."¹⁰⁶

Discrimination is that which occurs with the response but this is not just free will. "The essence of self-determination is discriminating one's own being *as it occurs*."¹⁰⁷ The opposite of this is "yielding to indiscriminate

---

103. *OBH*, 118.
104. *OBH*, 118.
105. *OBH*, 56.
106. *OBH*, 57–58.
107. *OBH*, 58.

impulses or desperately willing what is not attainable."[108] Adam practiced discrimination but not free will, for there is no free will in disobedience to God. The choice of Eve was made for him, but it was not a coercive choice. Eve was not forced upon Adam, for there was no other possibility but Eve. The actuality of Eve created her possibility. This was also true with the fruit in the garden. "The question as to which fruit could be eaten in such a way as to authenticate and complete the personal life of each could only be answered in this way: any fruit that God has set before you as a possibility. In this case self-enactment was completed by choosing and eating, not by questioning and reflecting."[109]

The question, What is the will of God for my life? can very easily create anxiety not hope, Anderson contends.[110] Besides this is our modern obsession for certainty. Are we sure we are "in" the will of God? What if we "miss the train"? To be led by God does not necessarily mean that we know the outcome in advance. Instead, "Christ leads us toward God's will as the outcome of our life, not from the standpoint of knowing God's will in advance."[111] "Free will" often tortures us as our spirits are wracked with indecision about whether or not we followed God's will. Anderson sees this as important even for Christian organizations that are very easily tortured by trying to discern God's will in terms of their plans.[112] "God's will is not the plan . . . but the outcome of the plan. In other words, you should not attach God's will to the plan but to the goal which the plan is designed to reach. God's will is what we discover at the end, not at the beginning."[113] "At the end"! Anderson's eschatology is sometimes subtle but it is still very profound. This is the distinction between the Christian's "destiny," which we can know, and our "vocation," which is liable to all sorts of random effects.[114] This is something that the anxious seminary student may not want to hear, worrying about God's "call," but which has some biblical precedent.

---

108. *OBH*, 58.
109. *OBH*, 59.
110. *SOG*, 189.
111. *SOG*, 183.
112. Cf. Anderson, *MGB*, 60–61, 81–85, 94–95, 116–31.
113. *SOG*, 184.
114. *SOG*, 188–89

The Christian prophets "through the Spirit . . . told Paul not to go on to Jerusalem" (Acts 21:4), which Paul did not heed! Paul did not claim to know the will of God, only that he was "constrained in the Spirit" (Acts 19:21) to go on to Rome and finally to Spain. Others did not want him to go, foreseeing trouble, but in the end all they could say was "The Lord's will be done" (Acts 21:10–14). "The will of God is the outcome of the plan, not the basis on which the plan is developed. The will of God is not something that we can use to make our plans 'fail-safe.' Nor is the will of God something that we can use to overcome our own inner sense of being led by the Spirit."[115] The prophets were right; Paul was arrested after he arrived in Jerusalem (Acts 23:23–24). Yet Paul did not see this as failing to follow the will of God. He wrote from jail, "What has happened to me has actually helped to spread the gospel, so that it has become known throughout the whole imperial guard and to everyone else that my imprisonment is for Christ" (Phil 1:12–13). We do not know if Paul ever reached Spain. "God does not 'overpower' our own moral will and free choice, though he 'leads' us toward the ultimate goal and good for each of us, and through his sovereign grace and power, upholds that as his will."[116] This does not confuse our "vocation" with the "calling" that every Christian possesses to be in Christ.[117]

God gives boundaries but not choices. "The divine command discriminates boundaries and limits, but not specific actions or choices, for human being. The freedom and responsibility to exercise discrimination as a single choice and action amid a multitude of possible choices is the basis for our own subjectivity."[118] Anderson's view is of particular relevance in our postmodern culture, where "multi-tasking" has evolved into "omni-tasking," a seemingly infinite number of choices available on the world wide web that can paralyze one from making any choice, or at least bedazzle and befuddle one into settling for knowledge when one needs wisdom. "Life is composed of a never-ending series of choices among many possibilities, each of which appears to be indiscriminate. This is true of our most significant choices (whom to marry, where to live, what career to prepare for) and of the most trivial ones (what to wear, which

---

115. *SOG*, 185.
116. *SOG*, 186.
117. *SOG*, 187.
118. *OBH*, 59.

dress to buy, where to go on vacation)."[119] Our subjectivity arises out of this discrimination, but this is discrimination *based on the reality that is presented before us,* not an ideal. Sin and pathology result when we hold out for the ideal, whether it is school, marriage partner, or house. "The discrimination of 'what is mine,' or what completes my own being, is not premeditated. It takes place 'as it occurs' in the course of our life. That it does occur is evidenced, not by its matching some abstract criteria, but because our being answers at the deepest level to the being of another. This 'knowledge' is inaccessible on a more abstract conceptual level; witness the often-heard statement: 'I don't see what she sees in him!'"[120]

Prayer, Anderson, argues, "is not a means of removing the unknown and unpredictable elements in life, but rather a way of including the unknown and unpredictable in the outworking of the grace of God in our lives."[121] I would put this statement on the list of Anderson's "greatest hits"! There are echoes here in Anderson of Bonhoeffer's belief that the ethical decision comes in the historical moment when one is compelled by historical events to act.[122] Adam and Eve are again instructive: "Adam did not wait to see what other females might offer him by way of possibility when God presented him with Eve, but seized that possibility as his own. For in that event he experienced the answer to his own being in her."[123] Romantic love, therefore, is relativized. "Someone may ask, Did he love her? Here too it must also be understood that love is the result of a good relationship, not the cause of it."[124] "Love is the result of a good relationship, not the cause of it." Another one of Anderson's "greatest hits"!

Anderson is most particularly concerned to embrace a view of subjectivity that is not subject to introversion but "outwardness." This is especially true in relationships of intimacy, particularly in marriage and the family. Secrecy in family relationships can be destructive. "The person who retreats from extrinsic subjectivity into the secrecy of inner life actually moves away from true subjectivity and tends to become impersonal and

---

119. *OBH,* 60.
120. *OBH,* 61.
121. Anderson, *JAJ,* 51. Cf. Anderson, "Judas as an Answer to Prayer" in *GAJ,* 53.
122. Bonhoeffer, *Ethics,* 222–24.
123. *OBH,* 61.
124. *OBH,* 61–62.

'mere' object."[125] God's word from outside posits our subjectivity, therefore the other is constantly before us. "Where the self is not re-posited in the series of interactions which necessarily make up existence in relation, subjectivity disappears and only impersonal and indiscriminate actions remain."[126] Love expresses itself because of the constancy of the relationship. Intimacy, therefore, does not create love. "Thus, in close friendships or marriage, it is not enough that certain actions take place which maintain the continuity of the relation. In these actions there must be a re-positing of the self in such a way that the actions are discriminate rather than indiscriminate."[127] What is at stake in the determinism vs. free will or grace vs. free will debate is not just an abstract issue, but what happens in a relationship. Is a relationship simply because of one's free will, the "free will" of an omnipotent God to do whatever he pleases, or the "free will" of the autonomous human being to "choose" obedience? Both of these views are challenged by discrimination, the proper response in any relationship of love, in which determinism or free will does not define the relationship. "The act of reaching and touching another person merely out of instinct, habit, or by compulsion is an indiscriminate act, even though it is an act peculiar or habitual to that relation. For discrimination is not achieved by habit, but through an appropriate congruence between act and being."[128]

Love, Intimacy, and Theological Anthropology

Why does love end?

> Love dies, not through lack of actions, but through lack of discrimination. That is, love is maintained as a positive quality in a relation by the re-positing of the self in such a way that encounter of being takes place. Many have testified to the tragedy that marriage can destroy a good relationship! What does the damage in such cases is not the exclusivity of the marriage vow which in some way usurps the freedom of the relation, but a loss of subjectivity which substitutes impersonal routine for discriminating personal ones. There is nothing so indiscriminate as familiarity.[129]

125. *OBH*, 62.
126. *OBH*, 63.
127. *OBH*, 63.
128. *OBH*, 63–64.
129. *OBH*, 64.

This paragraph from Anderson is quoted in full because it gets at the heart of his concern. Love is maintained through discrimination not simply attention. In fact, love is not even created by actions, even actions of intimacy. "For intimacy is earned through the sense of discrimination which is present in the relation. The greater the sense of discrimination the greater the level of intimacy."[130] So much of contemporary society believes we choose whom we love and create intimacy by "sacrifice" or "devotion." This is a romantic ideal, but it does not reflect a theological anthropology based on humanity as determined by the Word of God. "And again, by discrimination we mean the presence of being in the act, so that in the act of discrimination one is both vulnerable and also absolutely secure."[131] The theological roots for this are in one's doctrine of God, especially as expressed by Karl Barth and T. F. Torrance, that the being of God is known in his acts.[132] There should be no concept of God that is abstract power, just as there should be no doctrine of humanity that is abstract free will. Jesus Christ and his oneness with the Father (in the famous word of the Nicene Creed, the *homoousion*), reveals the being of God as he assumes, heals, and redeems our humanity. To be human is to be contingently related to this God, to be made in his image.[133] This leaves no room for a dualism between being and act in human relationships, particularly in marriage and the family.

Marriage as Sexuality in Contingent Commitment

If there is contingency in marriage, one is tempted nowadays to find all sorts of possible impediments; unfaithfulness, incongruency, one of the spouses "changing," the list seems endless. But the contingency that Anderson speaks of is the contingency created by the Word of God. Yet this is a word of belonging, not bondage. Is this possible?

Because co-humanity is expressed as male and female outside of marriage, marriage is not needed, according to Anderson, to "sanctify" or bring a moral order to the sexual impulse. "Because sexuality is set within

---

130. *OBH*, 64.

131. *OBH*, 64.

132. Barth, "The Being of God in Act" in *Church Dogmatics*, II/1, 257–71; T. F. Torrance, *The Trinitarian Faith*, 73; *The Christian Doctrine of God*, 4, 95, 149, 236.

133. *OBH*, 65–87.

the command of God in terms of authentic humanity, marriage does not constitute the basis for a sexual ethic, but itself comes under the true order of sexuality as co-humanity."[134] Covenant is that which provides the theological basis for marriage, not as a "contract" of two equals but as God's unconditional pledge toward the couple.[135] Yet couples hardly love unconditionally (though they may try). "The divine covenant is unilateral in its inception, and bilateral in its expectations. That is, the covenant was established only from God's side, but requires reciprocity on the part of humans."[136] There can be commitment, however, commitment that is not legalized by a wedding ceremony but by acknowledging God's commitment toward them.[137] "The person who sees marriage as the ethical validation of suspicious sexual inclinations might presume that the ideal is a totally nonsexual relationship prior to the wedding night. Those who hold this view tend to equate marriage with the wedding ceremony. However, for the one who sees marriage as the result of an encounter that involves mutual commitment to a life of covenant partnership, 'premarital' will mean something other than 'pre-wedding night.'"[138] This is the distinction between a "theological" and an "ethical" view of marriage.[139] As controversial as his views on sexual ethics may sound, does Anderson reveal how little theological thinking exists in evangelical circles on such practical subjects as sex and marriage? The covenant by God in the marriage is expressed, not in a deterministic decision by God that "these two" will be married, but by the doctrine of election. The "selection" by the couples becomes God's election.[140] Therefore, once the selection is made, the covenant binds them to God and to one another. "We discover our election in the process of our selections."[141] Again, the sexual act is not the determinative of marriage but faith expressed in the covenant of God, whenever that takes place for the couple. The "sin" can be found after the wedding ceremony as well; when the relationship is taken for granted, when the journey of humanization is not recognized, when change is not

134. *OBF*, 88.
135. *OBF*, 86ff.
136. *SOSN*, 7.
137. *OBF*, 92.
138. *OBF*, 93.
139. *OBF*, 86.
140. *SOSN*, 39–42.
141. *SOSN*, 40.

accepted. Anderson drolly comments, "My own observation is that when two people marry, the woman always expects the man to change but he never does, while the man expects the woman never to change but she always does!"[142] Anderson claims that marriage is not based on feelings or even the relationships but partnership in purpose. "Partnership marriage does not focus on itself, an earthly institution, but strives to transcend itself by focusing on a joint task."[143] But does Anderson end up sacrificing the relational for the *teleological,* the purpose, in contrast to the covenant God who has a purpose for Israel but does not simply love Israel because of its purpose?

Divorce and remarriage are not issues to be dealt with, then, apart from the contingent relationship to the Word of God. Denying that contingency and the presence of the living God of grace and forgiveness presents another mistaken use of rules for divine and contingent order, and a neglect of how theological anthropology dynamically intersects with ethics (Mark 2:23–28). The goal is neither divorce nor remarriage. But the divine Word as revealed and living in Jesus Christ, in his incarnation, is not bound by a *telos.* "God's purpose" can be an idol and can end up denying God's freedom in the actuality (not just the possibility) of a concrete, historical person, or couple.[144] Bringing in abstract law is a way to avoid participating in the continuing vicarious ministry of Christ: "Rather than hold persons accountable to God himself, and rather than be accountable to God themselves, ministers often take refuge in abstract principles that either excuse them from acting on behalf of those who are in need of support when going through the breakdown of a marriage, or free them to act in every case with little regard for the implications of their actions. In either case, they trivialize and render ineffective the commandment of God."[145]

Family as the Penultimate Contingent Relation to God

Theological anthropology gives birth to a theology of the family, in Ray Anderson's thought. What is a family? is not simply a sociological or ideo-

---

142. SOSN, 40.
143. SOSN, 207.
144. OBF, 112–13.
145. OBF, 102.

logical question, but an ontological one. In contrast to the twin naturalistic options of biology or culture, Anderson argues for "a natural or created contingent order."[146] Both advocates of the traditional nuclear, biological family and those that find themselves in a relationship of love because of apparently random circumstances are advocates for what they perceive to be "natural." Anderson proposes an alternative that is upheld by the divine Word, but not in a causative or mechanical way. No, "the quintessential order of the family" as contingent means a contingent relationship, as dependence on God, "an event that may or may not occur with regard to natural laws," but "is dependent upon something outside of its own structure of being, even though it has its own order and structure."[147] The reality of God is always that which upholds the human being and also the human family.[148] Therefore, there is a way to understand something that possesses an essential order yet is subject to change, "something old" and "something new," "the old commandment" that is also a "new commandment" (1 John 2:7–8).[149] Just as the form in the Old Testament changed with the New, the same love of God continued. "Because love is a quintessential structure of relationship, rooted in God's own being, the structure of social relationships remains normative even though the roles through which that structure is expressed change."[150] Contingency is the living relation to God, the God who gives commands out of love. "But when the commandments become detached from the quintessential purpose and are made into a law that claims absolute power in its own right, the commandment becomes an absolute form of the command of God."[151] This is how Jesus perceived the Pharisees' use of the Sabbath (Mark 2:23–28). The Word of God is always coming, coming out of the future, yet not based on human autonomy.[152] Yet, order is not the same as regularity or rules in its contingent nature. Therefore, one must not speak of the family as the "cornerstone" of society, as traditionalists do.[153] This would be to deny contingency. "The question facing us is not whether or

146. *OBF*, 17.
147. *OBF*, 17–19.
148. *OBF*, 18.
149. See the climax of Anderson's theology of the family in *SOSN*.
150. *OBF*, 18.
151. *OBF*, 20.
152. *OBF*, 23.
153. *OBF*, 24.

not the concept of family is becoming obsolete but whether the kind of family we experience leads us to be more or less human."[154]

The Bible speaks of the relationships between parents and children as essential, not an order of the family, because God himself is relational as Father (Eph 3:15; Isa 63:16; Matt 23:9).[155] The relational nature of parenting develops from humanity as determined by the Word of God; a becoming because it is a being.[156] Parenting involves the child's experience of belonging, not just anxiety, an event of humanizing.[157] The challenge for the church today is not just to defend the traditional family against modernity and postmodernity but to exemplify a "biblical" or "redemptive modernity" that presents a liberation, a humanization, and a re-socialization in the family that modernity has always sought but in the communal context that is sought by postmodernity.[158]

Death as the Ultimate Contingent Relation to God

The old woman lives in a cellar, always afraid of going out. For in this way, she reasons, she will never meet Death. She is old, but she does not want to die. But a soldier is shot and wounded outside her door and she reluctantly lets him in. She cares for him, bandages him, gets to know him, until he reveals himself to be Death. He has come for her, but first to alleviate here fear of Death, fear of the unknown. She walks with him outside.

Does this episode from *The Twilight Zone* television series speak against a Christian view of death as the "enemy" that must be vanquished (1 Cor 15:54–55)? Ray Anderson, following suggestions by Karl Barth, suggests that the Christian must see death as well as on the line of continuum with life, that there is a distinction between dying and death.[159] Anderson will have more to say about death in terms of eschatology, as we will see in the last chapter. Yet death and dying must be essential to our theological anthropology, Anderson contends. Dying is natural to contingent creatures before God. But death has made it unnatural, a judgment.

---

154. SOSN, 203.
155. OBF, 60–61.
156. OBF, 55.
157. OBF, 66–69.
158. SOSN, 5–10.
159. OBH, 135–40.

Our humanity as determined by the Word of God is not based on any possibility within ourselves but given by God, and that includes immortality.[160] "The presence of faith in the act of dying is a context in which dying becomes a pilgrimage rather than a dead-end. There is a 'living end' which reaches back into the experience of dying. The seventh day breaks into the sixth."[161]

Again, Anderson's doctrine of humanity under the Word of God as being both creatures of the sixth and seventh day is instructive. We are not determined by death, but we cannot blissfully ignore it and cling to a platonic doctrine of the immortality of the soul. As creatures of both the sixth and seventh days, we are upheld, not by a possibility within our immortal soul, but by the community of faith, an expression of humanity being essentially co-humanity. The church is involved in "contextualizing death in a community of faith and hope."[162] Therefore, the community should be intimately involved in those ethical decisions of the human being, its body, and the transition of the body toward death. We are not to be left to either natural law or even individual autonomy, as much as we might value both. "The natural transition from mortal creatureliness to immortal communion with God is meant to be a pilgrimage which is accompanied. Dying is meant to be contextualized in the form of a processional. Death is not an end, but the transition to a new beginning. . . . When we let go of the hand we do so with the deepest conviction of our souls that without faltering or fumbling someone else is taking that hand."[163]

"There is something destructive of our own personhood when we look away too quickly from the presence of the body of another in death."[164] Anderson's own connection with the death of his father and growing up on the farm kept him from that.[165] The rituals, the processional, the anointing, all are important. "There is co-humanity, even in the process of dying. The eschatological reality of the resurrection of the body is grasped from this side of life and the divine Word which sustains the human person in

---

160. *OBH*, 136.
161. *OBH*, 140.
162. *OBH*, 140–145.
163. *OBH*, 143.
164. *OBH*, 144.
165. *OBH*, 145. Cf. Anderson's relation with his father throughout *UW*.

unity of body and soul is made manifest."¹⁶⁶ Again, theological anthropology determined by the Word of God can resist the fatalism of creaturely destiny as well as the hubris of human self-will that rages and will not "go gentle into that good night" (Dylan Thomas). "I am not in a 'life-and-death' struggle, in which death can rob me of some hoped-for victory or prize."¹⁶⁷ "Faith, then, finally, is more fundamental than fear."¹⁶⁸

A Case Study to Consider: "Visitors to the Church"[169]

Facts and Dilemma

Visitors William and E. B. (not their real names) came to speak with Pastor Edgar about membership in Faith Church. They both come from conservative Christian backgrounds (William— Catholic and E. B.—Pentecostal, and a praise team singer), but they were asked to leave when it came out that they were gay. They are, in many ways, very traditional Christians, but they are also a "couple." They do not want to join what they called "a gay church"; they have visited such churches and did not feel comfortable there. Rather, they want to be a part of a traditional church that is welcoming to all. They also do not want to make people uncomfortable. They just "want a place to worship and serve," they said. The pair have been visiting here for some time, like the worship and messages, and feel very welcome. They do not want to cause the church or the pastor any problems, they said. They do not want to be ministers or officers. They hope some day to adopt children. Asking about the church's attitude toward homosexuality, Pastor Edgar shared with them the denomination's stance and the current debate. The pastor said that in this church they would find people at both ends of the spectrum on the issue and every place in between. He also said that "We do have some gay people here, but homosexuality is hardly their 'agenda.'" Pastor Edgar also shared that he struggles with the Bible on this issue and is married to a divorced woman, but that they have moved beyond that to accept God's grace and seek to love God and

---

166. *OBH*, 145.
167. *UW*, 113.
168. *OBH*, 145.
169. This case study was provided by an anonymous pastor.

neighbor. The pastor and the pair then prayed together. The pastor invited them to continue worshipping there and attend a luncheon for prospective members when they are ready. They are planning on attending.

Do you agree with how the pastor handled the situation?

Questions to Ponder

What are the implications for Anderson's theological anthropology in this case? Consider these thoughts:

1. "The problem of a non-theological anthropology . . . is not that the human person is the starting point, but that the human person seeks to have the final word, the decisive judgment, as to the nature of humanity." Is there an arbitrary understanding of sexuality in human personhood in this case?

2. Election speaks of the actuality of the human person that God creates in contrast to an "ideal" human person. "We can become human because we are in fact divinely determined to be human and *are* human." How is ministering to "crucified humanity" in this case different than promoting the "ideal" human person"? How is the goal of liberation and humanization different from perfectionism?

3. "There is something inherently tragic about the form of our present community of human love. No person is ever totally 'at hand' to us. Even if it should appear to be so in any given moment, there is an inevitability of separation and distance which each person must traverse." What is the place of the *tragic* in human sexuality and how should the church minister to this issue in light of the tragic?

4. "The absence of sickness is not yet health." Where is the goal of health in this case? How do we know what health is (implications of the humanity of Christ)?

5. "Creatureliness is an undifferentiated field upon which the occasion of the human occurs." Does creatureliness have implications for how we view our feelings about our own sexuality? What place does our creatureliness play in understanding our sexuality from a theological perspective? How does this contingently relate to the divine Word? Should the church promote or ignore our creatureliness?

6. Discrimination is different from determinism and free will. How would upholding humanity as determined by "natural law" or as essentially autonomous (free will) be different from what Anderson calls discrimination? Does that make any difference in our theological understanding of sexuality and how the church responds, especially if discrimination involves dependence on the community (implications of God as Trinity and co-humanity as social before it is spiritual)?

7. "Did the divine Word that summoned me into being as a human person—and therefore determined that I would be either male or female at the level of creaturely being—also determine an essential polarity for me? Is there an intrinsic order to sexual identity?" (See Gen 1:26–27.) If so, how is the church to encourage this? If not, what is the church to encourage when it comes to sexual identity?

8. "The church as the body of Jesus Christ expresses both divine preference and divine presence in the lives of its members." Can Faith Church do both with William and E. B.?

9. "The question facing us is not whether or not the concept of family is becoming obsolete but whether the kind of family we experience leads us to be more or less human." Does this have implications for William's and E. B.'s desire to adopt children? Should the church encourage this?

3

JESUS CHRIST, DIVINE RECONCILIATION, AND THE HEALING OF PERSONS

The Reconciliation by "The Little Man on the Cross"

FOR RAY ANDERSON, Christology and soteriology, the doctrines of Jesus Christ and salvation, like all of theology, are not to be considered abstractly and ideally, apart from real humanity and God's incarnation into real humanity, the humanity of Jesus Christ, so that we may really speak of the humanity of Jesus Christ as the humanity of God.[1] Humanity as co-humanity, as seen in his discussion of theological anthropology, speaks loudly to what often can be very abstract and speculative debates on the relationship between the divine and human in Christ, the place of the "historical Jesus," and the virtues and vices of various "theories" of the atonement.

The tragedy of Cain and Abel is Cain's failure, not to be his "brother's keeper," but to be his "brother's brother."[2] Often ignored, therefore, in discussions of social justice, are the implications of the classic dogmas of Christology and soteriology. Social justice talk in the church can easily degenerate into sloganeering and simply reflecting a contemporary political party's stand, whether on the right or the left. Anderson's alternative is refreshing. "Social justice is not an abstract principle, nor is it an ideal to be pursued. Social justice is the core of human experience. It is bread and water; it is blood and bones; it is brothers and sisters who unlearn

1. *SPT*, 314.
2. *SPT*, 311.

the knowledge of how to hurt and how to kill and who learn to live in the power, the freedom, and the hope with which God intended that we should live."[3] When Anderson explores social justice, he does not leave his theological anthropology behind. "If there is any theological basis for social justice, it lies between us, within our humanity; it is anthropological," connected to human freedom and the image of God in humanity.[4] Therefore, "social justice is a human, not merely an ethical, problem."[5] As he frequently does, Anderson distinguishes between "ethics"—that which only pits rules or logic about "the good" and "human rights"—and that which is particularly and concretely human.

In a short essay, "The Little Man on the Cross," Anderson tells the story of a woman who growing up Roman Catholic, had come into bad times, had entered a Christian bookstore asking for a cross to buy, but was dissatisfied. "Yes, I'm looking for a cross," she replied to the salesperson, "but do you have one with the little man on it?"[6]

"The little man!" Humanity, not just an abstract religious symbol, must be on the cross in order to avoid degenerating into just religion or ethics. So in Anderson's Christology, it is essential that the humanity of Jesus Christ be a particular humanity, the humanity of God in Jesus of Nazareth, which nonetheless has universal implications for all. Therefore, in the particular humanity of Jesus, God hears the cries of injustice against particular human beings, not just an abstract "humanity."[7] Salvation will include God's work against injustice, for "God's own dignity is at stake in ours, for we are in his image."[8]

Therefore, Jesus Christ is no one else than the humanity of God, borrowing from Karl Barth's thought. "Social justice flows not from the justice of God as an abstract principle but from his humanity as a historical and continuing power of reconciliation. It is not God's justice but his humanity that is our hope."[9] Abstract justice is not just neutral but malevolent, as Cain and Abel teach us. "We will kill each other out of

---

3. *SPT*, 311–12.
4. *SPT*, 312.
5. *SPT*, 313.
6. "The Little Man on the Cross" in *SPT*, 315.
7. *SPT*, 313.
8. *SPT*, 313.
9. *SPT*, 313. See Barth, *The Humanity of God*.

the abstract principle of justice. Cain could have argued that he was just in defending himself against his brother. His brother had taken away his rights. His brother had secured by some means the favor of God. 'No one has the right to take the favor of God away from me; that is unjust!'"[10]

The humanity of God is known in the vicarious humanity of Christ, which is not only where God "binds both the victim the oppressor to God," but is also a "continuing humanity of God in Christ" that "binds God to the cause of social justice from the side of those who suffer injustice."[11] As Anderson likes to say, if there are two sides to humanity, Christ will be found on the wrong side, the one rejected by others.[12] This is not an ethical categorical imperative however, but a recognition of suffering and abused humanity by the humanity of God in Jesus Christ, the ones that may be unknown to the world but are known by him (Matt 25:40).[13]

At the core of theological anthropology and social justice is belonging. Divine reconciliation is bringing that "belonging" back together. In Anderson's tales of his father, a farmer in South Dakota, he speaks of "unspoken wisdom" in his father's example.[14] A particularly poignant moment occurs when Anderson's father instructs the young Ray to put his hand into the farming soil and says, "Son, this soil is part of your life—you take care of it and it will take care of you."[15] What might be interpreted as simply an exhortation to remain as a farmer was interpreted broadly by Anderson in the years ahead to speak of belonging: to his father, to God, and to whatever soil in which he placed his hand.[16] Our disconnect created by sin is that which takes us away from such belonging. Divine reconciliation is meant to heal and reconnect our humanity, our very real, particular humanity, with relationships, with belonging. The distinctively relational nature of Anderson's theology of salvation, and indeed the whole of this theology, is obvious. This is manifest in the doctrine of God as well in which transcendence is radically transformed by the incarnation: "Like my father, God does not talk down to me, as a man to

---

10. *SPT*, 313.
11. *SPT*, 313.
12. *HTRG*, 253.
13. *SPT*, 315.
14. *UW*.
15. *UW*, 13.
16. *UW*, 18.

a child; nor does God attempt to treat me as divine with the pretense of 'God-talk.'"[17] This is "the transforming power of the 'we' of God."[18]

The Church of "The Little Man on the Cross" as the Place of Divine Reconciliation

We are not left with the option of a place of reconciliation outside the all too imperfect reality of the church. For the church is the *body* of Christ, and therefore very much the assembly of particular concrete human beings, persons who to some extent have been grasped by Jesus Christ. Yet this does not mean that the church is a continuation of the incarnation. "But the church is the place and the presence and power of the incarnate One who through his Spirit inhabits our humanity and leads us to meet his humanity in the world."[19] The church, nonetheless, "risks its own survival" as it sides with those who are considered to be "dispensable" by society, such as the elderly and the infirm.[20] Anderson is not going to wait for the latter doctrines to get around to discussing the church, as in so many Protestant theologies.

The Cross and Resurrection of "The Little Man"

"The Little Man on the Cross" is a powerful expose of what is often lacking in evangelical theories of the atonement. Evangelicals claim that the cross is at the center of the gospel. Yet what does the cross mean in our churches? "The cross in our churches is empty, stripped of flesh, disincarnate, hung on invisible wires designed by architects, suspended by engineers, in total ambivalence, ascending or descending somewhere between heaven and earth."[21] The unreality of our crosses is quite evident, corresponding to our lack of recognizing particular, concrete human beings encountering us and being encountered by God in the humanity of Jesus Christ. Anderson is quite blunt how concrete this humanity is: "Where are the little people on the cross? Go into the Laundromat on any urban

17. *UW*, 19.
18. *UW*, 19.
19. *SPT*, 314–15.
20. *SPT*, 315.
21. *SPT*, 316.

street corner after 8:00 some evening and note the mothers who are the sole support of their families there to do their washing with their little children by their side. Contemplate hospital beds on which people toss and turn and cry out in the night and become disoriented. Take a good look at the federally funded housing projects that are an embarrassment to the city but the only haven for the hopeless."[22]

"Too often, I fear, we have torn the cross out of the flesh and made it the symbol and servant of our highest religious aspirations."[23] Neon crosses, gold chained crosses, or even "old rugged crosses" can be worn without embracing broken humanity. "But the truth of the gospel is not just that humanity has been put on the cross; it is rather that the cross has been sunk deep into humanity. The incarnation has the cross on it before the incarnate One hangs on the cross."[24]

The cross of "the little man" is a reflection of the incarnation. Atonement must never be separated from the incarnation or else it just becomes that reflection of our highest religious aspirations. This is not a magic wand for humanity, but a magic nonetheless meaning that God has dug deep into our humanity, even estranged and rejected humanity, devastated by tragedy, injustice, and its own foolishness. "This is a true theology of liberation."[25]

Perhaps at the heart of the problem is what we expect "happens" with the atonement. This is a question Anderson wrestles in his provocative chapter, "Did Jesus Have to Die on a Cross?" in *Dancing with Wolves While Feeding the Sheep*.[26] He frames it in this way: Would atonement have taken place if Jesus died of a heart attack instead of on the cross?[27] Objections are immediately raised that this would not fulfill Scripture and satisfy the need for the "blood" of Jesus. But Anderson responds that what we might be leaving out of our theories of the atonement is the resurrection. Because it was "the little man on the cross," the cross has sunk deep into our humanity, so it is imperative that our humanity be raised with Christ; in that is atonement. "One must surely say that it was not the

22. *SPT*, 316.
23. *SPT*, 316.
24. *SPT*, 316.
25. *SPT*, 316.
26. *DWW*, 69–78.
27. *DWW*, 70.

Jesus Christ, Divine Reconciliation, and the Healing of Persons

death of Jesus the Son which satisfied God the Father, but his resurrection from the dead! It is life that God desires, not death."[28]

Atonement involves the giving of new life, in others words, not just the removal of guilt. The pastoral and practical implications of this are profound, perhaps explaining both why the doctrine of the atonement is so irrelevant to the Christian life of many and why so many Christians know they are forgiven but have no sense of spiritual power in their lives. Confession of sin and absolution might be performed in many churches (but a decreasing number in "contemporary" worship?) but with little effect on the congregation. "When the church pronounces forgiveness of sins and spiritual peace with God without also providing the power to overcome the effect of sins in one's daily life, this may not only be a liturgical fraud but spiritual malpractice."[29]

"Liturgical fraud!" "Spiritual malpractice!" These are stark, harsh words. At the root of the problem is, once again, our theological anthropology, the splitting of the spiritual from the physical, the soul from the body, sanctification from justification.[30] God is concerned with particular, whole human beings. The incarnation involves God taking upon the particularity of the body and soul of Jesus Christ in order to provide his life for our life, the "wonderful exchange" of which the Fathers and T. F. Torrance speak.[31] Atonement is not simply forensic, a declaration of forgiveness nor simply a moral inspiration, "We are to love like Jesus," but this is an ontological act, reaching into every point of our humanity, our deepest feelings as well as our deepest being. Therefore, the power of sin has no place to hide, even in a "secret life."[32] "Did Jesus have to die on a cross? Well he did, but it was not the crosspieces of a tree or the spilled blood which put an end to our sins. He didn't just bleed to death, he loved to death, and that love is alive and blowing freely through the Holy Spirit into our hearts to make us children of God."[33] Otherwise, the "liturgical fraud" and "spiritual malpractice" continues in the church through our

---

28. *DWW*, 74.
29. *DWW*, 75.
30. *DWW*, 76.
31. T. F. Torrance, *The Trinitarian Faith*, 179.
32. *DWW*, 77.
33. *DWW*, 78.

empty words of confession and exhortations to "be like Jesus," much to the frustrations and despair of the people.

Healing with God and Our Deepest Feelings

If reconciliation is conceived to be the goal of the atonement, then that reconciliation needs to deal with actual, particular human persons in relationships. Ray Anderson's sophisticated book masked as a popular volume, *Everything That Makes Me Happy I Learned When I Grew Up* seeks to provide an alternative to the popular book by Robert Fulghum, *All I Really Need to Know I Learned in Kindergarten* (1988). In contrast to Fulghum's thesis that we need to retreat to basic childhood lessons, Anderson sees our need in learning to become mature adults. In terms of salvation, Anderson is exploring the nature of the Christian life as salvation as maturation and not to be bound by obsessions with the unfairness of life; concerns that betray a lack of attention to human feelings by theologians and our misunderstanding of the reconciling power of the gospel. Salvation, and particularly sanctification, is to be understood as maturing, but not simply at intellectual (doctrinal) or behavioral (ethical) levels. Borrowing from the philosopher John Macmurray, feelings reflect who we are.[34] There is no use "spiritualizing" or "intellectualizing" the fact that it was I who was hit in the head with the baseball bat, regardless of whether it was an accident or a malicious affront! I was the one who was hit and I feel the pain! A Christian doctrine of salvation has to address the particular, actual human person that feels. The nature of the atonement should address us at every point in our humanity, including our feelings. So Jesus cries on the cross, "My God, my God why have you forsaken me?" (Matt 27:46). "Jesus could have blamed the devil and lashed out at his enemies.... Dare he charge the very name of divine love with turning away from him in his great hour of need? Yes, he would and he must. For we do not reach the core of our injured self until we demand of God an accounting for our soul's condition."[35]

Such a radical view of the atonement might stand in contrast for many to one that instead would demand for humanity to make an account of itself to God. That may be our basic religious instinct, but is this what

---

34. *SC*, 64.
35. *ETTM*, 59.

Jesus Christ, Divine Reconciliation, and the Healing of Persons

is going on with the cross? No, we are entering into the ministry of Jesus Christ that is not interested first of all in defending God. It is interested, rather, in hurting, desperate human beings, and taking their place and standing in for them in all their anguish. "And where is the relationship that will hear our complaint, tolerate our accusations and yet provide a source of healing?"[36] The perennial problem of innocent evil existing if a good and all powerful God exists, the problem of theodicy, needs to be faced by any theory of the atonement, especially if theology is to be the ministry of Christ. "When we split God off from his responsibility for evil in the cosmos, we have given as much power to the devil as to God."[37] (In other places, Anderson seems to say, however, that perhaps God is not able to do some things.)[38] "Trust is repaired only when the feelings most authentic to the self have been expressed and validated and we receive the affirmation that we are under the power of blessing rather than cursing."[39] The need of the infant is still there but we have been stymied so many times by others and by ourselves. One is needed to come before God in our humanity. The lament Psalms, Job, and Lamentations in the Bible all speak of the needs of the concrete, suffering human person. "We have been taught to express love and adoration to God, not anger and accusation. But this only reveals how far we have removed God from our deepest feelings. There can be no other point of beginning for the repair and renewing of our feelings than to direct them to God. Whatever our concept of God, we must discover the reality of God at the depth of our feelings."[40]

The child's pleasure instinct is not to be denied but one recognizes that the moment it is thwarted, unhappiness sets in.[41] A "moral right" to fulfillment can be challenged by the child whose toy car is taken by another. This continues in the adult life. The marriage turns out not to be what we expected. The joy of togetherness has become a stifling chokehold on our personal pursuits. It seems so unfair. Why would God allow this to happen? we ask. "If we can't trust God to give us what is good, what

---

36. *ETMM*, 59.
37. *ETMM*, 63.
38. *SC*, 184–85.
39. *ETMM*, 67.
40. *ETMM*, 61.
41. *ETMM*, 22.

can we trust? I feel betrayed, even punished."[42] Others seem to have happy marriages. As Anderson titles one chapter, "Someone Else Always Has More Toys: Life is Not Fair!"[43]

What is missing is seeing ourselves as objects of God's love, as those who are loved in a way that God desires for us to grow to maturity in spiritual as well as emotional ways. "The key to happiness is not to annihilate the self but to rediscover the self as an object of God's love. . . . The key to happiness is not gratification but self-fulfillment gained through delayed gratification, with self-worth and moral worth affirmed."[44] Jesus may want us to become like a child to enter the kingdom (Mark 10:15), but this is not the same as continuing to live in a childish manner. "It may well be that Jesus was reminding adults that they carry within them a childlike longing, which has become a childish bent toward controlling their own destinies and securing their own gratification through controlling others."[45] A simple yet constant refrain in Anderson is, Do we know that we are loved by God? Religion and moralism seek to deny our longings. Neither "can we dismiss unhappiness as an 'unhealthy attitude' for which the cure is repeated doses of manufactured pleasure."[46] Yet happiness should be sought, but not as an entitlement.[47] An entitlement is never grace but something we think we deserve because of "nature." Grace, in contrast, is freely given love in the midst of lives that are often not fair, free, or friendly.[48] Feelings "are not something that flow through a faucet, waiting to be turned on. Rather, feelings *are* the self and are crucial to its development from child to adult."[49]

Salvation and reconciliation must speak to us at the depths of our deepest feelings, at the level of our values, not just our beliefs.[50] Shared values and goals in a marriage are more important than shared beliefs.[51] This seems strange to us because we assume that a couple has a "Christian"

---

42. *ETMM*, 21.
43. *ETMM*, 15–25.
44. *ETMM*, 24.
45. *ETMM*, 25.
46. *ETMM*, 47.
47. *ETMM*, 10.
48. *ETMM*, 13–68.
49. *ETMM*, 68.
50. *ETMM*, 88f.
51. *ETMM*, 91.

marriage if they both simply believe in Jesus. But it is at the level of what we value that all relationships grow or are broken apart. For the most powerful drive in human life, Anderson contends, is self-fulfillment, that which goes back to our infantile narcissism.[52] A dualism between beliefs and values often develops that mask our deepest feelings and needs for self-fulfillment. Happiness can be seen to be a kind of salvation found in marriage, but a salvation that always disappoints. "When happiness becomes a goal in itself and an expectation placed on another person, we are doomed to disappointment."[53] This does not mean, however, that marriage is only a duty to be endured. "We *should* experience happiness in marriage, as well as in many other experiences and relationships in life. Marriage may be an occasion for the gift of happiness to be received, but it can never be the cure for unhappiness."[54] Anderson seems to be criticizing marriage as a kind of "pseudo-salvation" that we expect too much out of and are bound to be disappointed, but he refuses to disconnect self-fulfillment and happiness from God's reconciliation. "People do not walk away from their vows because they are bereft of faith, but because the value of their faith has shifted. Where once desire for each other empowered them to find value in their marriage roles, desire has fled, leaving only duty. In the end, desire will always win out over duty, for desire taps the fire that fuels faith and causes hope to be reborn out of despair."[55]

If the healing of the atonement includes the level of our feelings, then this is a suggestion that salvation, and the doctrine of the atonement, is wider and deeper than we have often been taught; it lies at our deepest level, *ontologically*, at the level of our being. Christian ministry needs to address the whole person at that depth, not just be satisfied with behavioral change. So Anderson can speak of "salvation/atonement" as the "healing of the self."[56]

The ontological root of the atonement is Jesus Christ himself. "Health . . . is not the absence of sickness, but a positive orientation of the self toward the objective hope which results from God's initial intention."[57]

52. *ETMM*, 91.
53. *ETMM*, 101.
54. *ETMM*, 101.
55. *ETMM*, 102.
56. *OBH*, 172–75.
57. *OBH*, 173.

Salvation, as well, is not just the forgiveness of sins, a legal declaration that one is "off the hook" but union with Christ, sharing in the life of the Healed One. "Christ is not merely a healer, he is the healed one. He took on himself the diseases and infirmities which inflict humankind and made an end of them in the resurrection from the dead. He is the source of health because he himself has been made health for us even as he was made sin for us."[58] Christ's vicarious act is not just a vicarious death, but a vicarious *humanity*, so that we can be bold enough to say that Jesus himself was "healed," that is, he took upon all of our disorder. Atonement is ontological, not just behavioral or forensic.

Anderson is careful, however, not to equate all sickness with sin. Because atonement is ontological it includes the entire being, sickness and sin, but they are also differentiated. "Salvation is healing because it is an eschatological act, and as such, forgiveness of sins includes the restoration of that which is human."[59]

As healing, the atonement has an ecclesiological but not necessarily religious context, since it involves the whole person. There is a ministry of both "ordinary" and "extraordinary" exorcism in the church.[60] We might recognize the dramatic function of extraordinary exorcism in the casting out of demons. But we often ignore that there is an ordinary exorcism of the Christian community "casting out" that which is inhuman from its members through the reality of the community of reconciliation. Election as the affirmation of the self is an affirmation of what is truly human. Ordinary exorcism is an act of excluding that which God does not elect in our humanity, not just maintaining ethical boundaries in the church. Positively, ministry involves not just exorcism but also edification because atonement affects the whole person not just one's disorder. Being confronted by Jesus means that not only is the demon cast out, but also results in one sitting at the feet of Jesus "clothed and in his right mind" (Luke 8:35). "The fundamental problem of human personhood is thus shown to be ontological rather than behavioral."[61]

---

58. *OBH*, 173.
59. *OBH*, 173.
60. *OBH*, 174.
61. *OBH*, 175.

Grace Seeks No Excuses

If divine reconciliation extends to our deepest feelings, that does not mean it is a pleasant experience. Ray Anderson remembers well his mentor, Thomas Torrance, and his words in an Edinburgh classroom: "Grace must first kill before it can make alive."[62] Grace is not just "accepting that you are accepted" (Paul Tillich), something that is only warm and pleasant. The biblical narrative of Abraham and Sarah stresses that Sarah's "barrenness" is just as important as Abraham's faith.[63] Despite Abraham's desire to have Ishmael as the chosen one (Gen 17:18), the son who came forth from Abraham's desire to "help" God, God's grace first works with the barrenness of Sarah. It was not that the Lord was confronted by Abraham's unbelief but by his false belief, his belief in his own potential, not the contrast between obedience and disobedience but "true obedience as compared with false obedience."[64] Peter rebuked Jesus when he was told of Jesus' fate. "God forbid it, Lord! This must never happen to you!" (Matt 16:22). He was not an unbeliever; but he believed, his convictions were wrong! Those to whom we preach and teach in the church are usually not without some kind of belief. "When we preach the Word of God, we are speaking to those who believe in something dear to them, and to those who rely on their own way of obedience. This belief must be stripped away as was Abraham's belief in Ishmael."[65] Abraham cries to God, "O that Ishmael might live in your sight!" (Gen 17:18). "What is difficult, as we hear it in the plaintive cry of Abraham, is the death of our own Ishmaels. The grace of God must first kill before it can make alive."[66] It is important to note that for Anderson it is grace, not the law that kills, in contrast to Luther.

Grace, however, is not restricted to salvation history. Grace exists in the Garden of Eden. "Grace was there in the garden, where there was neither fear nor guilt. When grace is conceived as only a remedy for sin and a response to human disobedience, it makes grace a secondary movement within the being of God. And, in a strange twist, it makes human sin the occasion by which grace comes."[67] From the beginning, grace exists

---

62. *SOG*, 97; *SOM*, 47.
63. *SOM*, "The Grace of God Which Presupposes Barrenness," 43–51.
64. *SOM*, 47.
65. *SOG*, 101.
66. *SOG*, 97; *SOM*, 47.
67. *SOG*, 98.

as that which we cannot comprehend by human logic, so we cannot fit the God of the Bible into a "worldview," which only becomes "our own scheme of how things should be."[68]

Yet the "inner logic" of grace and barrenness does not preclude human involvement. "Human obedience and faith are not set aside by grace, but are drawn into the grace of God as an indispensable aspect of God's ministry."[69] Grace does not perfect nature, but it does not fight against nature. "Grace is not a supernatural addition to a natural life, but the empowering of natural life to realize and produce a divine potential."[70] Anderson refuses to accept a dualism between the natural and the supernatural: "We only know the grace of God when we experience the presence and power of God as a supernatural source of what we experience in our natural lives."[71] Anderson's refusal to deny the place of self-fulfillment in his theological anthropology is very much related to this kind of thinking. But can Anderson avoid the charge of *synergism*, that salvation is part the work of God and part the work of the human? He seems very close to this at times. "The righteousness reckoned to Abraham was not based on his passivity, but on the fact that he actively grasped the promise as coming through sexual union with his wife, Sarah. Isaac did not drop down from heaven, but came through the cooperation and participation of both Abraham and Sarah."[72] It might be unfortunate that Anderson uses the word "cooperation," for that seems counter to any place for barrenness, but his concern is not to destroy the mystery between grace and free will, which the word "participation" avoids much better. Similar to the Virgin Mary, she did not simply "cooperate" with God but participated (Luke 1:38) in what God was going to do as said by the angel (Luke 1:30–31). "Once again, the virgin womb of Mary, the mother of Jesus, is the *ex nihilo* that grace presupposes in order that the ministry of God be authentic."[73] The key is the difference between Isaac and Ishmael. "The difference between that which is produced through the grace and power of God and that which is not cannot be located in the degree of human participation

68. SOG, 99.
69. SOG, 102.
70. SOG, 102.
71. SOG, 103.
72. SOM, 50.
73. SOM, 51.

and effort, but solely in that which grace produces through the human act."[74] Ultimately, grace is not a substance, supernatural or natural, but God himself in Jesus Christ. As Anderson comments on Col 1:27, "Christ in you, the hope of glory" . . . "dwells within us, not just *through grace,* but *as grace.* Christ is the content of grace."[75]

Grace "kills" in order for us to press on to maturity. The problem, as Anderson frequently recounts, is the refusal to grow up, to become an adult, to "press on to maturity" as the Bible teaches (Heb 6:1; Eph 4:15). That can only be done in marriage when a shared vision or goal is embraced. "Desire, however, must be attached to a vision and goal that can be realized only through sacrifice and commitment. This is not child's play or childish pleasure."[76] Feelings of no longer being in love should not be denied. But what do these feelings indicate? "And what feels like the loss of love may actually be the costly separation of self-gratification from self-fulfillment."[77] We can often have desires that we confuse with blessings that we are entitled to from God. "From the very beginning, our longings get mixed up with our needs. When we attempt to fulfill a longing by satisfying a need, the hollow space in our heart grows larger. Blessings belong to longings, not to needs."[78] Divine reconciliation, Anderson seems to be suggesting, includes the reconciling of the self to oneself, moving from infantile self-gratification to a mature self-fulfillment that includes articulating visions and goals and being empowered to live by the delay of gratification, that is, by faith and hope.

Our culture, Anderson contends, is increasingly child-centered.[79] Guilt-ridden parents desperately try to attend every one of the child's soccer games. In contrast, Anderson observes that he learned to become an adult because his father invited him to increasingly participate in adult activities. Does our culture then simply encourage children to remain as children? Do parents, often overworked in families supporting two incomes, end up maintaining the child in a children's world rather than preparing them to become an adult? Anderson acknowledges the differ-

---

74. *SOM,* 50.
75. *SOG,* 104.
76. *ETMM,* 102–3; cf. *UW.*
77. *ETMM,* 103.
78. *ETMM,* 117.
79. *UW,* 67.

ence between the urban and the rural culture, and the changing times. Nonetheless, his argument is that "children are likely to develop their own convictions about life and values from observing the actions of their parents and other adults in their own world."[80]

"Pressing on to maturity" is not just a moral exhortation but a reality of grace. Anderson sees this in the example of his father's confidence that the young Ray can ride the horse ("Ray can do it!"), an empowerment of self-confidence based on grace. "The test was no longer my ability to avoid that horse, but my faith—my confidence—in my father. To beg off from riding would show that I had no confidence in my father's judgment.... What we call self-confidence is not based on our ability to perform, but on the trust we have that our performance will *not* be the sole basis of our acceptance and value to others."[81]

This is in contrast with those who have to constantly perform before their parents in order to continually earn and maintain their love.[82] "Trust is giving someone the freedom to fail in order to grow."[83] This involves learning the place of personal responsibility, somewhat difficult in a piety that presumes that God causes every move in one's life. "Taking responsibility for one's life and one's failures is not to deny the role of God in life. I have no trouble with a God who admits that humans were placed in a dangerous world with little skill to navigate life's treacherous corners. I have more difficulty with a God who would take over completely and not show me how to take responsibility for my actions."[84]

Living by excuses is a way, ironically, of living legalistically, not by grace. "If our excuses are accepted, we feel acquitted of wrongdoing. By offering excuses, we are saying that we should not be held responsible for our action or lack of action."[85] We assume that grace is the same as living by excuses. Anderson might be saying that would be ignoring the "belongingness" of grace. Grace binds us to God and then to one another, not as an excuse to be irresponsible; to God, others, or ourselves. Grace wants to bring back together, to reconcile. "Forgiveness is never the granting of

---

80. *UW*, 67.
81. *UW*, 24.
82. *UW*, 24–25.
83. *UW*, 25.
84. *UW*, 35.
85. *UW*, 45.

Jesus Christ, Divine Reconciliation, and the Healing of Persons

an excuse, for in that case, there is nothing to forgive. Real forgiveness—which is a gift, which is grace—says, 'Your life counts and I send you forth to finish the job!'"[86]

Only having received grace, from God and others, can we then sacrifice for the sake of others. "The value of love can be measured only by what it costs, what we are willing to lay on the table and trade away for the sake of the transparency and vulnerability of looking another person in the eye and saying, 'My soul is bound on this earth to our common destiny. I desire above all else to gain my soul. And I give you your freedom from my deepest needs in order to have my greatest desire.'"[87]

This is a learning process, certainly, which reminds us that salvation involves not only justification but also sanctification. "The value of patience, kindness and giving way to the other must be learned."[88] "The search for self and for fulfillment during adolescence and early adulthood is derailed when a belief system is added on rather than developed with regard to personal values."[89] I think I have seen that tendency in some students that seem to want to perpetually live as a teenager in a church or student "youth group," never really having been equipped to become Christian adults. So salvation is not simply providing a religious but a human need. "I am now convinced that we gain the abiding power of faith when what we believe to be true is received into the self as a gift of God that meets the deepest longing for self-fulfillment. Faith does not create its own value over and against the value of the self. Rather, faith transforms the value of self-fulfillment from its childish grasp on what is immediately at hand to the abiding value of what is achieved through the giving over of self to longer-range personal goals."[90]

When Jesus spoke to the woman at the well (John 4:1–15) by addressing the passion in her relationships, he was not simply invalidating passion by promising "living water" which would become a spring of "eternal life." "He touched the core of this woman's passion, which up till that moment had been indiscriminately poured out in a series of unfulfilling relationships. What others may have seen as a promiscuous sexual

---

86. *UW*, 48–49.
87. *ETMM*, 105.
88. *ETMM*, 104.
89. *ETMM*, 92.
90. *ETMM*, 94.

passion Jesus diagnosed as an unfulfilled thirst for a love that gave back as much as it took."[91] In other words, faith as the response to the salvific act of Christ does not simply give us a new religion that invalidates our humanity. This has profound implications for how the Christian does counseling, as one example. What exactly is the goal of counseling, making one religious or humanizing?[92]

Faith Is in the Seed, Not the Harvest

What is faith? What does it mean to respond to grace by faith? How is faith related to ministry? These are crucial questions for Ray Anderson. Using another story from his relationship with his farmer father from that remarkable book, *Unspoken Wisdom: Truths My Father Taught Me*, Anderson suggests that "faith is in the seed, not the harvest."[93] He observes retrospectively that his father was never depressed by a crop loss. Why did he not go into deep depression, quit farming, and shake his fist at God? This involves the nature of faith.

"Our deepest feelings are often invested in that which has the capacity to break our hearts."[94] Another "greatest hits" saying from Anderson, I would say! In other words, faith, in a crop or in a relationship, always has that potential to fail. Faith (including prayer) is no guarantee of success. But often we live by whether or not there is a successful "harvest." However, as Anderson says, "Those who live by the harvest may die by the harvest."[95] Our hope should be in the planting, not in the harvest, for we cannot control the harvest.[96] Faith, in contrast to many of our ideas and practices, does not guarantee that we are in control. Quite the contrary. "When we sow in the soil, we invest our time, energy, and limited resources in the power and promise of life. This is as good a definition of faith as I know."[97]

---

91. *ETMM*, 96.
92. See *CWC*.
93. *UW*, 50–59.
94. *UW*, 53.
95. *UW*, 51.
96. *UW*, 53.
97. *UW*, 54.

Jesus Christ, Divine Reconciliation, and the Healing of Persons

How does one "strike back" then from adversity? Anderson cites a line from a poem by Edna St. Vincent Millay, which speaks of a farmer rising from his crop failure "with twisted face and pocket full of seeds."[98] The farmer will plant again with the new seeds, but not with ignoring the devastation of what has happened; he goes on "with twisted face." "We should never forget this. Hope always emerges out of the ruins of some failed dream, some unfulfilled desire, some loss that must be grieved" in contrast to a childish or superficial hope.[99] The seed must be sown, but beyond that, the matter is in God's hands.[100]

Faith does not need to "murderously" seek proof. Anderson tells his family tale that at every Christmas Eve, the cows stand up like the cows in the manger in honor of the Christ child![101] But, as a child, Anderson was never tempted to go out into the barn to see if that was true. That would be going out of doubt not faith. The "truth" there was different; a truth that cannot be easily told, and if told, only by stories.[102] "There are truths that can be received only by faith."[103] Anderson muses on what this might have meant for the apostle Paul, one who had never seen Jesus in his incarnate ministry. Should he have gone to see if he could find Jesus' bones in a tomb? "I doubt that Paul ever made a pilgrimage to see Jesus' empty tomb for himself or visited the place where Jesus was said to have been born. Yet he told the stories about what happened in each place a thousand times. If he ever had been tempted to 'see for himself'—just to make sure—I would bet that he paused and whispered to himself (as I did at the window on that Christmas Eve): 'Careful, Paul. Once you go, it will never be the same.'"[104]

Anderson is not endorsing credulity in faith. It does make a difference that Jesus was raised from the dead. But *how* we know that will say much about our respect for the uniqueness of the event as well as our understanding of the nature of faith. Faith does involve knowledge but a knowledge that reflects our humanity and the nature of God, a knowledge

---

98. *UW*, 54.
99. *UW*, 55.
100. *UW*, 58.
101. *UW*, 118–24.
102. *UW*, 121.
103. *UW*, 122.
104. *UW*, 123.

that reflects the divine-human reality of Jesus Christ.[105] As such, its mystery needs to be maintained and nurtured, not torturously reduced to evidences that do not fit its object. As Anderson's mentor, Edward J. Carnell, says, faith is a "resting of the mind on the sufficiency of the evidences."[106] Anderson comments, "In saying this, he stressed the fact that it is not the *kind* of evidences that warrant faith, but the *sufficiency*."[107] The question for the Christian, from Paul to Luther and Kierkegaard, is always, "Is faith, not absolute certainty, enough?" Is there an "epistemology of faith" (and of grace!)? Faith in God, however, is not a kind of "gnostic" faith but more like learning to trust someone.[108] "I have come to believe that the concept of 'saving faith' or 'Christian faith' is a wrong way to think of faith. While there certainly are aspects of faith that are so extraordinary that one can speak of having the 'gift of faith' (1 Cor. 12:9), there is a generic kind of faith that is characteristic of a person who has learned to trust, to love, and to remain faithful despite adversity and even disaster."[109] Once again, this is normally taught by parents. Divine reconciliation, in other words, is not such a fantastic category that our humanity is overrun by divine action. Anderson respects the person whom was taught by one's parents to trust. He believes that God respects that one, too. This is not the Catholic doctrine of "grace perfects nature," but it christologically embraces the human and does not destroy the human. Still, there is much here for rich dialogue between Catholic, Protestant, and Orthodox.

Living by the Contours of Grace and Faith, Not by the "Straight-Row"

Ray Anderson, coming out of American evangelicalism, has a particularly strong reaction against legalism of all forms. Believing in absolute truth often makes absolutes out of everything, especially morals. Again, Anderson's concern for theological anthropology is evident. Morals are about how we treat people. A "straight-row" approach (another farming

---

105. See Barth, "Faith as Knowledge," *Dogmatics in Outline*, 22–27.
106. Carnell, *Christian Commitment: An Apologetic*, 76.
107. *SOG*, 152.
108. *SOG*, 152.
109. *SOG*, 152.

analogy) imposes one's will on the soil.[110] The legalist does that with people, becoming "rigid and intolerant" of anything that promotes "change and novelty." "When we view life from this perspective, we invest a good deal of energy and time in straightening and correcting," becoming "perfectionistic and judgmental."[111] In addition, "straight-row persons also use the whip a good deal on themselves. Self-punishment can become a goad to greater effort as well as a penalty for failure to measure up. Chronic anxiety is a by-product of such an approach to life."[112] In contrast to straight-row farming is contour farming. Contour farming respects the lay of the land and seeks to follow the nature of the land. This may not be the greatest efficiency in an age that glorifies efficiency, but efficiency can become especially hurtful when we are dealing with human beings.[113] Treating the contours of persons is different. "This means investing time and effort to examine the contours of another person's hopes, wishes, fears, insecurities. It means putting aside 'efficiency' and the paradigm of straight-row thinking, with its rigidity, perfectionism, and stubbornness."[114] The contour approach will appear chaotic and inefficient to the straight-row legalist. Yet in terms of human beings, it will respect the particularity of persons whom are the goal of divine reconciliation, the real humanity that the Word of God assumed and redeemed.

Sanctification is the doctrine of the Christian life, often viewed as subsequent to the act of justification. Anderson turns the tables around, and thus offers a different perspective on living by grace and faith. Building upon Karl Barth's idea that Christ is both our justification and our sanctification, Anderson suggests that sanctification comes before justification.[115] Christ is the one who was first sanctified by the Father, who was even called by the demons, "the Holy One of God" (Luke 4:34; cf. John 17:19). "This is the basis for the sanctification of humanity. Sanctification means consecration through relation to God who is the holy One."[116] Jesus is the Justified One because he lived a life of perfect faithfulness and obedience to the Father. The verdict of the Father was

110. *UW*, 73.
111. *UW*, 74.
112. *UW*, 76.
113. *UW*, 78.
114. *UW*, 78.
115. *SOM*, 102–5.
116. *SOM*, 102.

demonstrated in raising Jesus from the dead "who was handed over to death for our trespasses and was raised for our justification" (Rom 4:25). "By virtue of his resurrection, Jesus Christ is both the justification and sanctification of humanity. Both justification and sanctification are to be found in Christ."[117] Our justification is based on his justification. This is true for sanctification as well, but he lives a life of sanctification *before* his declaration of justification by the Father through raising him from the dead. Yet without justification Christ's life of sanctification would only end up in death and hell.[118] "Jesus was, we may say, justified by faith alone. His resurrection was the verdict of the Father as the eschatological basis for his historical faith."[119] Resurrection, again, is an essential, eschatological element to the atonement.

The implications of this for the Christian and our view of sanctification are profound. Both sanctification and justification rest on "being in Christ" (1 Cor 1:30).[120] Jesus makes this clear in his high priestly prayer to the Father concerning his disciples: "As you have sent me into the world, so I have sent them into the world. And for their sakes I sanctify myself, so that they also may be sanctified in truth" (John 17:18–19). Therefore, "our faith is not in the objective fact of our justification, but in the God who raised up Jesus and who has given us assurance that we too shall be raised 'with Christ.'"[121] Our tendency is to locate both justification as in "my faith" and even more so, sanctification as the acts by which (even with God's help) I make myself "holy." At bottom, Anderson is seeking to redirect justification and sanctification from their usual roots in thinking based on legal pardon (justification) and what can become a nervous, anxiety ridden search for personal holiness (sanctification) into a christological reality that is relational, the Christian being found "in Christ," that favorite Pauline idiom.[122] However, has Anderson provided enough of a connection between Christ the Sanctified One and our process of sanctification? This will be important to ponder when he does treat the place of spiritual formation in the Christian's life, a subject of great interest in recent years (see Richard J. Foster, *Celebration of Discipline*).

117. *SOM*, 103.
118. *SOM*, 103.
119. *SOM*, 104.
120. *SOM*, 104.
121. *SOM*, 105.
122. *SOM*, 105.

Jesus Christ, Divine Reconciliation, and the Healing of Persons

Living by Values and Virtues, Not by Beliefs and Rules

Anderson expresses his shock and even dismay when he comes to realize something taught by his colleague, Dennis Guernsey: "marital compatibility depends more on shared values than shared beliefs."[123] This is shocking for a Christian who assumes the importance of sharing the same doctrine as Christians; if one does not do so, then it can be obvious that the marriage will be on shaky ground. But what Anderson comes to see is the practical importance of our values over what we say we believe. "Two persons may have quite different beliefs but share common values. Values represent the choices we make concerning spending money, investing time, and deciding what will give the greatest satisfaction."[124] The husband may live a life that values order and perfectionism; the wife, though, may be an adventurer who constantly seeks new experiences. Without a common goal, their values will constantly cause friction.[125] "In our contemporary culture, personal values have become separated from beliefs. Values have become related more to existential needs and desires than to the intrinsic worth or merit of a belief."[126] Immediate gratification is the value that trumps a society of whom 90 percent say they believe in God or a Divine Being from whom they seek guidance and help. Again, self-fulfillment should not be denied as the most powerful drive in human beings.[127] "The search for self and for fulfillment during adolescence and early adulthood is derailed when a belief system is added on rather than developed with regard to personal values."[128] Faith is not just cognitive assent but learned by the trust others have given to us and the values that have been passed down from generation to generation. "People do not walk away from their vows because they are bereft of faith, but because the value of their faith has shifted. Where once desire for each other empowered them to find value in their marriage roles, desire has fled, leaving only duty. In the end, desire will always win out over duty."[129] Again, this is why the doctrines of salvation and atonement so often become irrelevant to Christians in

123. *ETMM*, 88.
124. *ETMM*, 89.
125. *ETMM*, 103.
126. *SOSN*, 11.
127. *ETMM*, 91.
128. *ETMM*, 92.
129. *ETMM*, 102.

the midst of life's messy problems, unless salvation and atonement are seen as embracing the whole person because the whole person has been embraced by the vicarious humanity of Christ.

So also, spiritual formation will involve the seeking of virtues, those characteristics we admire in other people.[130] This is something very basic in a theology of the Christian life. "The formation of Christian character is not achieved by the teaching of Christian doctrine alone, nor by setting down rigid rules of moral discipline. . . . The critical moral experiences which contribute to the formation of character do not take place in the church, but in the family and in the daily lives of people in their primary relationships."[131] Virtues, therefore, are not an individualistic project for self-improvement but that which grows out of relationships exhibiting unconditional grace. One example is courage: "Courage is not measured by how great a risk or fear one takes; rather, it is measured by the degree of self-confidence one has as a result of the encouragement of others."[132] In contrast to fearlessness, courage is not based on avoiding fear. "Courage is more humble and far more realistic. It accepts fear as a necessary part of life. Without courage, fear would never permit us to open the door to life and love. It takes courage to hope to have faith when we know fear. It takes courage to live with our weaknesses, our vulnerability, our loneliness. It takes courage to live with fear."[133] Again, doctrines of salvation and atonement need to address the whole person, including at the level of our feelings, including ours fears, to create a genuine healing that reflects Jesus Christ as both the Healer and, amazingly, the Healed One.

Judas as an Answer to Prayer: Is There a Limit to God's Grace?

The ultimate example of one whose "beliefs" fail him is Judas. Therefore, Christians seem to universally say, he has disqualified himself from grace and heaven. But is this true? Is there a limit to God's grace? This is the theme of two of Anderson's most controversial, yet most popular books, *The Gospel According to Judas* (subtitled: *Is There a Limit to God's*

130. *LSBL.*
131. *SOSN*, 18.
132. *UW*, 28.
133. *LSBL*, 40.

Forgiveness?) and *Judas and Jesus: Amazing Grace for the Wounded Soul*.[134] Forgiveness is at the heart of divine reconciliation. But how far does it go in the light of gross evils and injustices? Is there much in the world that embraces "cheap grace"? Anderson daringly presents a fictional encounter between Jesus and Judas after Judas' death. What would they say to each other? Is there any grace for the "Judases" among us, the scapegoats that we conveniently find in every group, even in the church? We think that we are too much like Judas ourselves, like the inmate that wrote Anderson, identifying with Judas.[135] Anderson found this written once in a restroom in San Francisco; "Judas Come Home—All is Forgiven."[136] Dare the church say that?

At the heart of this is a problem with our doctrines of the atonement. Why do Christians who believe that they are forgiven by the blood of Christ still live in shame and powerlessness? Is it because our understanding of divine reconciliation does not include the whole of who we are as human beings, including our emotions and feelings, especially our deepest pains, such as in shame?[137] "This is why forgiveness can be a superficial salve that does not penetrate to the depths of the pain."[138] Many are repulsed by the possibility that some might be saved without knowing Jesus Christ as lord and savior in their lifetime. But this ignores the significance of the death of Jesus for all. "Death as the enemy of all persons has been overcome in the death and resurrection of Jesus Christ. . . . This is not a declaration of universal salvation outside of personal knowledge of Jesus Christ. However, it is an assurance that God, not death, determines the fate of the living."[139] We will consider this provocative thought again in our last chapter on ministry and the future of Christ. Anderson keeps us hopping!

---

134. While Anderson speaks of *Judas and Jesus as a* "sequel" to *The Gospel According to Judas*, "delving more deeply into the dynamics of God's grace" (JAJ, 9), most of *GAJ* can be found in *JAJ*. One wonders if the recent publicity concerning the ancient gnostic document of "The Gospel According to Judas" influenced Anderson to "reissue" *GAJ* within this "sequel," in part to avoid further confusion in what had already become a controversial book.

135. *JAJ*, 23.
136. *JAJ*, 9.
137. *JAJ*, 39.
138. *JAJ*, 10.
139. *GAJ*, 86.

In Anderson's fictional scenario, Judas, the one who betrayed Christ, yet also hung himself in remorse, is, after death, trapped in the loneliness of despair, not wanting to see the resurrected Jesus at all; that would make it only worse: "Go away! I have enough pain without your love punishing me further."[140] "Judas was tormented by the unknown quality in his life."[141] Jesus is just a reminder of Judas' failure.[142] Jesus responds that one cannot betray unless there is a relationship of love to betray. "Judas," Jesus addresses him, "betrayal is the sin of love against love. Unlike other sins, betrayal uses love to destroy what is loved."[143] The high occurrence of domestic violence is a tragic example of this.[144] We assume that betrayal means the end of a relationship, but that is not so. Because betrayal uses love, it implies the relationship. "We tend to magnify failure, in others as well as in ourselves, because we so often look at the effects of sin rather than at the wonder of grace."[145] On an interpersonal level, we often restrict divine reconciliation to that which can be forgiven. Our inability to forgive simply stops us because God does not only forgive but he is merciful. "Human forgiveness has its limits ... If forgiveness is not always a possibility, mercy is."[146] However, does Anderson here too quickly create a gap between God's forgiveness and the dominical imperative to "forgive our debts, as we have also forgiven our debtors" (Matt 6:12)? Still, should even the exhortation to forgive be viewed as something we can do apart from prayer since it is in the context of the Lord's Prayer, and is not just a bare moral exhortation? We can be merciful even when we are not yet able to forgive because to be merciless is to become inhuman.[147]

Shame is that which is created as the result of betrayal because shame, unlike guilt, comes forth out of a community. "Shame is a loss of our place with others and so is felt as loss of being. For being is dependent upon how others view us. Those who have the power to create our history have the power to make us feel worthy or unworthy at the core of our

---

140. *JAJ*, 13.
141. *JAJ*, 24.
142. *JAJ*, 17.
143. *JAJ*, 13.
144. *JAJ*, 42.
145. *JAJ*, 27.
146. *JAJ*, 29.
147. *JAJ*, 29.

being. More than guilt, it is the deep sense of shame, with its sense of loss of personal being, that drives many to suicide."[148]

So Judas is rarely given any credit for his remorse. Peter denied the Lord three times and he is embraced. The disciples all fled Jesus at the cross. Yet Judas, even in the commentary in Scripture, becomes the object of the shame that the early disciples must have felt. "Shame-based people find it difficult to forgive. They seek to compensate for their sense of shame by punishing others."[149] All institutions—family, church, and business—are desperate to find a scapegoat.[150]

Anderson uses Judas and Jesus as a way to include prayer into the reality of divine reconciliation, and therefore to bring in spiritual formation as a part of the doctrine of the atonement. Jesus prayed all night to the Father and in the morning he chose the disciples, including Judas (Luke 6:12–16). Judas was an answer to prayer! Often readers respond that this is only because Judas was a part of God's "plan." But do we really want to say that Jesus' prayers were not genuine and petitionary to the Father, asking for wisdom and guidance, and not just a foreordained fatalism? (At the very least, one might claim that God "foreknew" what Judas was going to do. But that still leaves a question about prayer and its efficacy.) Jesus is the one who taught, "Ask and it will be given you" (Matt 7:7). Is Judas then a cruel joke from the Father?

At this point we come deep into the risky nature of the trinitarian mystery of prayer. Anderson imagines Jesus saying to Judas, "I did not pray so that every decision might be to my advantage, but so that I might love every decision as affirmed by the Father who loves me."[151] Jesus prays to the Father in the Spirit. This trinitarian relationship speaks of belonging and intentionality. "Whatever the consequences of Judas's act, it cannot erase this fact, his life is no longer his own, but belongs to the Father and the Son. As an answer to prayer, Judas has been grasped by an intentionality that cannot be shaken by his own act of betrayal."[152] Judas is threatening to us because we, too, do not want to take the risk of a love that can fail. "We know too much of Judas, because we know too much

---

148. *JAJ*, 39.
149. *JAJ*, 40–41.
150. *JAJ*, 42.
151. *JAJ*, 16. Cf. "Judas as an Answer to Prayer" in *GAJ* (1991), 41–55, (1994), 43–55.
152. *JAJ*, 48.

of our desperate urgings and darkest fears. We're afraid when we get too close to the failure of any relationship. We keep our distance because, like the impulse to retreat from a good friend who ends a marriage we had a stake in, we fear it could happen to us."[153]

God's love has taken the risk that it may not be embraced by a welcome response, but that is the nature of genuine love.[154] Anderson's doctrine of God is in evidence here. He is not the controlling, sovereign Force that coerces us to love him. He takes risks. So when Jesus prays in this way this is not to "guarantee" that the Father will give him the "ideal" disciples. The Father does not give the ideal disciples but he does give the right ones, and that includes a betrayer, Judas. "Prayer is not a means of removing the unknown and unpredictable elements in life, but rather a way of including the unknown and unpredictable factors in the outworking of the grace of God in our lives."[155] The will of God is not simply a preconceived plan that we need to plug into. "What we discover, instead, is that the will of God is grounded in his promise as to the outcome of our lives, not in a detailed plan that remains hidden in the mind of God."[156] Again, our "selection" becomes God's "election." Yet this is not without a christological focus. The resurrected Jesus is the living Jesus. "As I grow toward health and wholeness I believe that the resurrected Jesus will explore with me the still unopened doors and dispel unknown fears."[157] This resurrected One is also human, with a human faith that prayed to the Father. Anderson imagines Judas possessing a "gospel" that he can bear witness to after his post-mortem encounter with Jesus: "It was strange. He did not try to talk me out of my despair and torment; he merely touched it with his own suffering."[158] He then can move on from trust to belief.[159] What we can hope in is the love and faith of Jesus. "When our love has been destroyed and our faith in prayer exhausted, as it was for Judas, then our only hope is in the love and faith of Jesus. He does not come because we have prayed rightly and loved perfectly; but he comes into our prayer-

---

153. *GAJ*, 89.
154. *JAJ*, 50.
155. *JAJ*, 51.
156. *JAJ*, 52.
157. *GAJ*, 128.
158. *JAJ*, 118. Cf. *GAJ*, 149.
159. *JAJ*, 119.

less nights and loveless days to become, once again, God's answer and a focus for our faith."[160] This is one of the most beautiful statements I have ever found on the vicarious humanity of Christ.

Anderson's consideration of the relationship between grace and faith is crucial here. Does our lack of faith disqualify us from grace? "When we view God's grace as conditional upon our perfection and success in living by his commandments, we will tend to use prayer as a way of securing God's promises by meeting the right conditions."[161] Our faith becomes the center, not grace. "In this view of God, a failure to produce a result through prayer throws us back upon our own lack of faith or, even worse, some spiritual defect that lies unconfessed and sabotages God's work."[162] Jesus responds to Judas, "What counts, Judas, is not our foolish choices, but my Father's gracious calling."[163] Personal choice has always been important in American evangelicalism, given its historical roots in revivalism, from the "sawdust trail" of tent revival meetings to Billy Graham crusades. Yet Anderson sees a fundamental practical and pastoral problem when our choices are viewed as the fulcrum of salvation. In effect, by submitting to conditions we are creating our own means of atonement and bypassing the atonement of Jesus Christ.[164]

Is it too much to surmise that Jesus actually knew when he chose him that Judas would be the betrayer? Indeed, Luke's account of the Last Supper makes it clear that Jesus knew that in giving the bread and the cup to Judas he was giving it to the one who would betray him (Luke 22:21). What this means is that Jesus' obedience counts more than even Judas' disobedience. Jesus says to Judas, "My destiny was to do the will of the Father, and I was obedient—even to the point of death upon the cross. Your betrayal did not put me there. You can't take away from me what is truly mine!"[165] Judas' (and our) belief is that we have been to the place where God cannot go. This may especially be seen in Judas taking his own life. Jesus responds, "And you think that by taking your own life you sealed your fate and plunged into the realm that God has forsaken? I have

160. *JAJ*, 53. Cf. *GAJ*, 54–55.
161. *JAJ*, 51.
162. *JAJ*, 51–52.
163. *JAJ*, 18.
164. *GAJ*, 20.
165. *JAJ*, 19.

been to the God-forsaken place, Judas; it was on the cross, not in the black hole in your own soul. One death in a God-forsaken way is enough; I have died that death—and behold I am alive!"[166]

Spiritual Formation as a Family Ministry

Anderson is wary of speaking of spiritual formation as an individualistic project. That would violate his belief in the essential nature of humanity as co-humanity. Some talk of spiritual formation is in his estimation in terms of "an inner rather than outer spiritual life, which is also more individual than social."[167] Rarely is spiritual formation portrayed in terms of a theology of the family. The fact that it is not betrays the lack of ontological attentiveness in our doctrine of the atonement and the lack of relevance of the atonement to spiritual formation since we do not view the atonement as the healing of the entire person in community. "For this reason, spiritual formation, as a task assigned to the process of being human, is not the imposition of an alien or parochial imperative upon otherwise complete human beings," an "extracurricular task" in the church.[168] Spiritual formation, in other words, is not just a religious but a human task. And as human, it takes place intentionally in the family. The purpose of spiritual formation is not just to produce religious behavior in a more heightened way or a greater quantitative amount. "What anthropologists call 'religious behavior' could very well be produced by a stimulus response mechanism at the creaturely level. I myself have seen a pet poodle taught to 'say its prayers'!"[169] I might add that recent attempts to locate a "religious" segment of the human brain are just as suspicious from a theological perspective. What is religious is not necessarily of God, as Karl Barth constantly reminds us.

Spiritual formation is not to be set apart from our humanity. "What is termed 'spiritual formation,' as an imperative and discipline of Christian life and faith, is correlated with the developmental process by which individuals mature as human beings."[170] Normally, that is in the context of

---

166. *JAJ*, 20.
167. *ETEC*, 61 n.3.
168. *OBF*, 116.
169. *OBF*, 117.
170. *OBF*, 118.

the family, as much as the family is involved intentionally (but maybe not consciously!) in teaching faith, hope, and love. Again, Anderson's father is cited as an example of what faith is about apart from "saving faith." "I learned to have faith long before I developed Christian faith. I was mentored in faith by my parents, not through their own 'confession of faith' articulated in the liturgy of the Lutheran church (though I do not discount the value of that!), but through their 'being faithful' in fulfillment of their task of life."[171] "Liturgy" is not to be restricted to the formal worship in the sanctuary but involves the family as well. The family is involved in liturgical acts that reinforce belonging and commitment. Growing up, one "must come under a form of 'tutelage' by which intentionality is learned through the rituals and habits of family or community life."[172] The pilgrimage of faith is simultaneously a growth in becoming an adult. The family and the church can help that, in training us to become mature and adult, or hinder that, even in what appears to be nurturing ways but whose security and protection only postpones adulthood.[173] "Whereas in love there is liberation from the self to live for and from the other, in faith there is liberation from the paralyzing and immobilizing fear that arises in the face of life's uncertainties."[174] To be a disciple is to follow Jesus the Son, not simply in obedience to ethical or ideological principles, but in sonship as "the ontological source of Jesus' love for the Father."[175] This means embracing those who are not lovely in the eyes of the world. So spiritual formation is not desperately seeking to become an "ideal" family, at least in appearance to others, but embracing hurting humanity along with "the little man on the cross." That this is rarely found is a scathing indictment of the church. Yet the church is always saved by the remnant:

> Who will teach the child born with a twisted body that life is a gift to be accepted and valued? Who will bring a child who once saw clearly to see the goodness of a life to which he is now blinded? Do you doubt that it can be done? Then you have not known the same people that I have known. Is bitterness and defiance more human in the face of deprivation than forgiveness and acceptance? Is harbored resentment at life's unfairness and manifest dissatisfaction

---

171. *SOG*, 152–53.
172. *OBF*, 121.
173. *OBF*, 125.
174. *OBF*, 126.
175. *OBF*, 123.

with one's own life more spiritually mature than a cooperative and loving spirit? No. Then why is the Christian religion so powerless to transform such lives through proclamation and teaching? Because unrealized hope cannot be healed by words that do not touch the pain and emptiness we all feel to some degree.[176]

Anderson's answer is not just an exhortation to get more spiritual or religious but to acknowledge how God uses our "co-humanity" in the process of being conformed to the image of his Son. "Good parenting and a participation in family life that itself is a liturgical reenactment of the created and redeemed order must do this."[177] God has become human in Jesus Christ and now we know we cannot and should not despise that humanity but see the grace of God reconciling it to himself, even in such an ordinary and often despised way as the family. The church is next, often as equally despised. Anderson has hope for both, because God has become human.

A Case Study to Consider:
"Staff Abused by Pastor"[178]

Facts and Dilemma

Carl (not his real name) had accepted a position as Director of Operations at a fast growing urban congregation, Hope Church. It was a very dynamic ministry with high-energy praise and worship and a very charismatic pastor, Pastor Doug (not his real name). The view of the ministry from the outside was very impressive, inviting to anyone. However, behind the scenes, it was a ministry plagued by humiliation, degradation, fear, and intimidation, all brought on by the pastor upon his own staff. As Director of Operations, Carl was responsible for ensuring the efficient operations of the entire ministry which consisted of about eighty different ministries. Carl was also responsible for overseeing all program management, the facilities maintenance, and was the next-in-charge after the assistant pastor. Carl's days mainly consisted of one meeting after another.

176. *OBF*, 128.

177. *OBF*, 128.

178. This case study was provided by Joe Barthell, a graduate student in ministry at Friends University.

Jesus Christ, Divine Reconciliation, and the Healing of Persons

The ministry was a very busy ministry in that it held three services on Sunday mornings, an additional service one Sunday evening of each month for communion, Wednesday night Bible study, a "Friday Night Alive" service, new members and discipleship classes every Saturday morning, three major conferences throughout the year, yet the staff got only one day off per week. In addition, the pastor expected his main staff members to be at every service and every event hosted by the church. Carl began to feel the toll when he felt he could not find the time to read and study the Bible or spend quiet time with God anymore. Not only did his relationship with God begin to suffer, but his relationship with his wife as well.

It was after joining the staff that Carl found out that Pastor Doug was to be one who ruled and managed people through intimidation and fear. When a staff person failed to do things the way he wanted them done, he would publicly humiliate them from the pulpit or in the staff meetings. Although he would not call the staff person's name in public, most everyone knew of whom he was alluding. For example, a project was started of building new risers in the balcony area of the church so that people sitting on the back row would be able to see the pastor better. This required removing all the chairs from the balcony to another part of the church. The chairs were very neatly stacked near the entrance to the church without blocking the entry but Pastor Doug had a problem with it because they were not returned back upstairs in preparation for Wednesday night's services only to take them down again the next day. The pastor, while preaching that evening, publicly threatened to fire Carl. He later publicly threatened to fire another staff member for missing one of his services. His attitude toward his staff either led them to being hard on those whom they supervised or to become so overworked that they would eventually burn-out. As a result, the ministry staff had a very high turnover rate.

Eventually Carl suffered from burnout and resigned after fifteen months of working there. Apparently no staff member, including Carl, had ever approached Pastor Doug about his leadership style and abuse of his staff. After resigning, Carl was left with guilt, shame, and the pain of wondering how he could have allowed himself to become susceptible to such abuse.

What does this situation reflect and could Carl have dealt with it in a better way?

READING RAY S. ANDERSON

Questions to Ponder

What are the implications of Anderson's doctrine of reconciliation for this case? Consider these thoughts:

1. "Social justice is not an abstract principle, nor is it an ideal to be pursued. Social justice is the core of human experience. It is bread and water; it is blood and bones; it is brothers and sisters who unlearn the knowledge of how to hurt and how to kill and who learn to live in the power, the freedom and the hope which God intended that we should live."

2. "Yes, I'm looking for a cross, but do you have one with the little man on it?" How is the pastor ignoring the humanity of Christ and how does that relate to his staff?

3. "Like my father, God does not talk down to me, as a man to a child; nor does God attempt to treat me as divine with the pretense of 'God-talk.' . . . [This is] the transforming power of the 'we' of God."

4. "The cross in our churches is empty, stripped of flesh, disincarnate, hung on invisible wires designed by architects, suspended by engineers, in total ambivalence, ascending or descending somewhere between heaven and earth." Why can the pastor live with the "ambivalence" in his ministry? ("Too often, I fear, we have torn the cross out of the flesh and made it the symbol and servant of our highest religious aspirations.")

5. "When the church pronounces forgiveness of sins and spiritual peace with God without also providing the power to overcome the effect of sins in one's daily life, this may not only be liturgical fraud but spiritual malpractice." How does this case reflect splitting the spiritual from the physical, the soul from the body, and sanctification from justification?

6. "Christ is not merely a healer, he is the healed one. He took on himself the diseases and infirmities which inflict humankind and made an end of them in the resurrection from the dead. He is the source of health because he himself has been made health for us even as he was made sin for us." How does the pastor neglect this? How can Carl find help in Christ as "the healed one"?

7. A "straight-row" approach (the legalist) imposes one's will on the soil. The legalist does that with people, becoming "rigid and intolerant" of anything that promotes "change and novelty." "When we view life from this perspective, we invest a good deal of energy and time in straightening and correcting," becoming "perfectionistic and judgmental." How is "contour farming" different? What would "contour ministry" look like in this case?

8. "Betrayal is the sin of love against love. Unlike other sins, betrayal uses love to destroy what is loved."

9. "Shame is a loss of our place with others and so is felt as a loss of being. For being is dependent upon how others view us. Those who have the power to create our history have the power to make us feel worthy or unworthy at the core of our being. . . . Shame-based people find it difficult to forgive. They seek to compensate for their sense of shame by punishing others."

II. ON MINISTRY AS THEOLOGY

4

MINISTRY AS REAL PRESENCE

A Sacramental and Relational Reality

FOR RAY ANDERSON, not only does *theology exist as ministry* (our beliefs about God must never be divorced from the continuing ministry of Jesus Christ) but *ministry exists as theology*; ministry is not simply practical "how-tos" but the continuing ministry of Jesus existing in the church that does not forsake the world. Anderson is fond of quoting Jesus in his high priestly prayer to the Father: "As you have sent me into the world, so I have sent them into the world" (John 17:18). There should be no separation between the ministry of Jesus and the ministry of the church. That may seem pitifully obvious, but the lack of the recognition of this fact is all too evident in the history of the church and in contemporary ministry.

Community has always been a reality not just a theory or slogan for Ray Anderson. This did not stop with his ten years as pastor in Covina, California, before he pursued his Ph.D. In taking the faculty position as professor of theology and ministry (note the combination!) at Fuller Theological Seminary, Ray and his wife Mildred joined his former parishioners Pete and Luanna Young and others in Huntington Beach, California in a small church they named Harbour Fellowship. Anderson was the pastor with the proviso that he could only pastor as preacher and lead a Wednesday night Bible study because of his responsibilities at Fuller. Committees were out and "ministries" had to be left to the handful that would venture on Sunday to a school multi-purpose room. Anderson would arrive each Sunday, with communion table packed in the trunk of his car, and meet the informally dressed twenty or thirty gathered. Gathering in a circle, a sermon by Anderson would be followed by sharing prayer concerns and distributing the Lord's Supper to whoever wandered in that Sunday. So Harbour Fellowship existed for over twenty years, "the high of the low churches," as Anderson jokingly referred to it. This was nonetheless a genuine theological laboratory, a community in which Christ was present, particularly for those in the area that had been burned by the established churches. Most did not stay long, inevitably looking for churches that had programs for their families, but Harbour Fellowship became a kind of "half-way house" for those scarred by religion and desperately needing the grace of Jesus Christ. This certainly included many of Ray's students at Fuller Seminary, many whom were skeptical of any reality of community in the church. As professor of theology and ministry, Ray Anderson never ceased to be a pastor while he was a seminary professor. It showed!

At the heart of a trinitarian-incarnational theology is the real presence of Christ. So much is at stake with this that we must see beyond the centuries of sacramental haranguing between Protestants, Catholics, and Orthodox. All Christians believe that Christ has risen from dead, that he is alive today. Anderson invites us to engage "real presence" as a theological center not just as a bone of contention.

Community as the Sacramental and Liturgical Place for Personhood

As Protestants should not be afraid of the sacramental, they should not be afraid of the liturgical. We need to be a liturgical church, Ray Anderson argues, but maybe not in exactly the way most advocates of "liturgy" think!

A sacramental reality is not just elaborate rituals but involves such mundane things as eating. The Lord's Supper, the Eucharist, the Mass, is a meal, and therefore an act of community that reinforces personhood.[1] "Hospitality is a greater miracle than teaching, for in it truth becomes

---

1. *OBH*, "A Liturgical Paradigm for Authentic Personhood," 181.

actualized so as to effect new dimensions of personhood."[2] Baptism is a communal act that signifies that human personhood counts.[3] These are not just acts remembering or in honor of Jesus, but acts of his real presence, for Scripture speaks of Jesus as the *leitourgos* (minister) who serves in the sanctuary of God (Heb 8:2). His own baptism is the action of identification with sinners.[4] "He is the liturgist, who chooses the fields, the shops, and the streets as his sanctuary in which to render service to God. As the incarnate Son of God, he takes humanity and brings it back to its appropriate serviceableness to the Creator."[5] As Calvin would say, the act of the partaking of the Lord's Supper is a real presence through the Holy Spirit that lifts us up with Christ to be seated with him in heaven.[6] The Ascension of Christ, an often neglected doctrine, is therefore essential to worship and Christology.[7]

The incarnate Jesus is the liturgist, meaning, however, that liturgical life cannot be restricted to the sanctuary. Sacramental living involves all of life, not just the religious, Anderson contends, much in agreement with the Quaker emphasis on all life being sacramental.[8] Anderson will continue to embrace the traditional Protestant sacraments of baptism and the Lord's Supper, but only as they are understood in the wider context of the ministry of Jesus the liturgist, the one who continues to do "rituals of reinforcement" through his community the church.[9] It is at this place that we need to consider the church.

Community is not just a slogan but a reality that expresses the life of the triune God, Father, Son, and Holy Spirit, known through the incarnation of the Son. "Thus, liturgy takes place as a fundamental experience of God as a fellowship of being. Divine service takes place within the Godhead: the Son serves the Father, and the Father confers his own

---

2. *OBH*, 181–82.
3. *OBH*, 179–80.
4. *OBH*, 181.
5. *OBH*, 181.
6. John T. McNeill, "Introduction" to Calvin, *Institutes of the Christian Religion*. Volume 1, lxiv.
7. See Dawson, *Jesus Ascended*, 106–58.
8. Trueblood, "A Sacramental World" in *The People Called Quakers*, 128–47; Pearson, *Notes on the Sacraments*, 3–4.
9. *OBH*, 181.

being upon the Son."[10] Many so-called sacramental acts can take place only because they are tradition or duty-bound. Just because a clan is present, or a group of like-minded individuals, does not mean that this is the community of Christ. "Community is more than a social event. It is the re-enactment of the personhood of Christ himself (his body), and the manifestation of his own service (*latreia*). This ongoing ministry of Christ through his humanity continues through the human community as his body."[11] The church, therefore, has a being that is sacramental and liturgical at its core. "This is the ontological grounding of the church as the people of God."[12] But this is not a power to dispense salvation. It is always contingent upon Christ.

Anderson tells the story of the church member, "Joe," standing outside the church, drunk, as the congregation is gathering for the communion service. This is both a tragic and a laughable moment; should the drunken church member be allowed to take communion? The pastor, as Anderson tells it, approaches Joe and says, "Joe . . . this is exactly the place you should be. When we gather, it is the Lord that is the host of the table, and we are all present as needy persons. I want you to come in with me and be with us."[13]

Another example of "cheap grace," where "all is forgiven"? Or do we have here a more sophisticated view of sacrament than we have often been taught, a view that is not disconnected from Christ as the primary sacrament, as the one who continues to live and minister in the same way as he did 2000 years ago? Do we really believe in the "real presence" of Christ, regardless of our denominational loyalties and practices? "Jesus is the sacrament of saving and sustaining grace that flows through the 'sacramental' acts of Baptism and the Lord's Supper, as especially constituted for the church, as well as through the very existence of the church itself as the sacrament of forgiveness and healing."[14] The church is a sacramental reality as it participates in the continuing ministry of Christ. "The church's life is thus sacramental in the sense that it is the continuing life of the historical Jesus ministering to the world on behalf of God while, at

---

10. *OBH*, 182.
11. *OBH*, 183.
12. *OBH*, 183.
13. *SOM*, 166.
14. *SOM*, 168.

the same time, the church is the eschatological presence of the coming Jesus Christ who has destroyed the power of death and gives assurance of resurrection and forgiveness through the Holy Spirit."[15] The issue, then, is not whether we are "sacramental," but are we sacramental *enough*?

Anderson is not afraid to speak of human beings as spiritual but he is hesitant to ascribe ontological status to *religious* human beings. This is true in the way that he can speak of *Spiritual Caregiving as Secular Sacrament,* a book that provides a non-religious "sacramental" basis for those involved in vocations of human caregiving.[16] The sacramental can often create a dichotomy between the religious and the secular, so that a constant tug-of-war exists between the religious and secular worlds. Most importantly for the Christian, how does the church embrace care of human beings, such as in counseling, which may not be "religious" but nonetheless perhaps help people more than their preacher's sermons? This is an issue Anderson addresses in detail in his book, *Christians Who Counsel.* In *Spiritual Caregiving as Secular Sacrament* he names this as a "secular sacrament." This is not, however, to divorce religion from spirituality. One interpretation of Anderson might be to say that religion has a *contingent* relation to spirituality. "Persons can thus be considered as spiritual/secular beings who express spirituality and experience it humanly, temporally, and at times religiously."[17] Like the Quakers, affirming that all of life is sacramental, all caregiving can be said to be spiritual. "It is in this sense that I suggest we view all authentic human caregiving as essentially spiritual (whether or not ostensibly religious) and that the *care* given by the caregiver be considered a *sacrament* in a secular (not primarily religious) sense."[18]

Adherents of the traditional view of sacraments, Protestant, Catholic, or Orthodox, will immediately protest that this separates sacrament from the church. Anderson responds with a christological basis, again borrowing from Karl Barth. Revelation coming into human reality is in the humanity of Jesus Christ, so Jesus Christ is the First Sacrament.[19] "Where Jesus is present there is grace, because he is himself the sacrament through

---

15. SOM, 170.
16. SCSS, 174.
17. SCSS, 174.
18. SCSS, 174.
19. Barth, *Church Dogmatics*, II/1, 54ff.; SCSS, 174; SOM, 167–69.

which grace flows. The sacrament does not precede the presence of Jesus, as though it could manipulate and dispense grace."[20] This fits nicely with Anderson's theology of Christian community: The first community that Christ creates is not the church but the "kenotic" community of sinners and publicans, sitting at table with them (Mark 2:15).[21] We will delve into this more in detail in the next chapter on "Ministry and Mission." Suffice it to say, this may be Anderson's most important contribution to ecclesiology, and may be his most important contribution to theology, period. The first community that Christ "empties" himself into (the word *kenos* in Phil 2:7: "he *emptied* himself, taking the form of a slave"), the "flesh" that the Word became (John 1:14), was fallen human nature, sinners and publicans, not religious people.

Spiritual caregiving becomes a secular sacrament in real, concrete, particular ways. Anderson tells the story of visiting Colin, in the last stages of a terminal illness.[22] Glancing at his watch, thinking how much time he had with Colin before he had to leave for his next appointment, Anderson realizes that he already had an agenda for Colin. He knew already what Bible verses and prayers he was going to share. The real presence of Christ is sacramental, he reflects, when Colin's humanity determines the agenda. In a kind of "reverse vicarious humanity," Anderson puts himself into Colin's place. Admitting to Colin all that is taking place, the meeting of a man who is well and a man who is terminal, Anderson concludes by saying, "Colin, you are doing something that I have never done. You are dying. You are facing the loss of everything that made life meaningful and good. I will have to do that someday. I am not sure how to do that. You are doing it well. I am here to learn from you. I need that wisdom. I want you to talk with me about what it is like, what faith and hope is like for you now. Tell me the truth."[23]

That which is sacramental is not just a power of the church but that which is relational. Like Bonhoeffer in recognizing that one must respect the "penultimate" moment if one believes in the "ultimate," then there is a time that must be silent and sit quietly at the bedside as well as a time

---

20. *SOM*, 167.
21. "The Kenotic Community" in *HTRG*, 227–38, reprinted in *TFM*, 302–14.
22. *SCSS*, 176–77.
23. *SCSS*, 177.

to speak the words of justification.[24] Anderson realizes that approaching Colin with just his "religious" credentials is far different from meeting him at a shared, spiritual level, in the same way that Jesus met the woman at the well, asking from her a drink of water. Sacramental ministry is that which asks, not that which demands. How would the ministry of the church be different if it had such a consciousness?

Community as Not Only Sacramental but Also Relational

As the community of Christ, the church is not only sacramental but also relational, as Anderson demonstrates in his visit with Colin. Therefore, along with the living Jesus, it admits brokenness into its sacramental reality. "All of Europe is baptized; so what?" Karl Barth was somewhere heard to say. Baptism can often be a duty-bound tradition, even a ritual of the state in Europe, with no community significance, unless it is seen as baptism into Christ, and therefore as baptism into a community. "The significance of these liturgical events which belong to community can be found in the way in which they are not only signs of being in Christ, but they also effect authentic personhood through repeated acts of community life."[25] Potluck suppers can be sacramental; but not necessarily so. There is no place for the *ex opere operato* of the medieval church, in which the sacrament works automatically apart from a community of care. This is also a judgment on "contemporary" attempts to make worship "relevant." "This is why genuine liturgical acts in the life of community do not depend on novelty for their effectiveness. The act itself is more than a repetition of a movement; it is a re-enactment of a reality and therefore a present experiencing and knowing of that reality."[26]

The relational nature of incarnational ministry can be quite a challenge to any church that finds its meaning in its religiosity. "Being a priest is precariously close to being a clown," Anderson provocatively suggests.[27] "Far too often, in our attempts to be priests, we end up only being clowns. Holiness occurs in the street, not always in the temple. Wherever humanity finds itself, no matter how tattered and torn, no matter how lost and

24. SCSS, 176; Bonhoeffer, *Ethics*, 146–70.
25. OBH, 183.
26. OBH, 183.
27. OBH, 191.

forlorn, is where liturgical acts should take place. For here there is vulnerability, here it counts."[28]

Ministry as relational is seen paradoxically in Ray Anderson's most private writings. Written originally while a pastor in the early 1960s, Anderson used this journal to write down some "musings" that perhaps his congregation wouldn't quite know how to take! Eventually published as the book, *Soulprints* (with some pages included in *Dancing With Wolves While Feeding the Sheep* and *The Soul of God*), these jottings are theological probings that relate the soul of the pastor with ministry at a deeply personal and intimate level, and thus are more "relational" than is our often superficial talk about "community" in the church.[29]

The Polanyian dictum that our being is conditioned at its root by its belonging is a critique of those who argue for Jesus Christ as the "God-shaped" vacuum in the heart.[30] If you grow up belonging, there is no vacuum that believing fills. "The problem with a vacuum is that it is indiscriminate and will draw in anything that is floating in the air."[31] In another favorite Polanyian quote, "We know more than we can tell," Anderson finds the depths of relationship. "There is a knowledge at the core of the self for which we will never find words. It rises up within us without our bidding and cannot be forgotten or erased by the most strenuous act of the will nor by the most delirious ecstasy of emotion."[32] There is something sacred about the other. "The human spirit is the core of the self as desiring, cherishing, longing, and believing. . . . To share our spirit is to receive the other into the sacred shrine of what is most personal and dear; to share the spirit of the other is to be welcomed freely and trustingly into their holy of holies." [33] In knowing another intimately there is simultaneously a deepening of mystery. "Intimacy is the intensification of otherness."[34] This otherness in relation is poignantly reflected upon in a poem that he calls "The Wall," where his solitude becomes paradoxically the opportunity for

---

28. *OBH*, 191.

29. *SP*; "Musings of a Maverick Theologian" in *DWW*, 123–46; "The Soul of a Preacher: A Kierkegaardian Diary," in *SOG*, 31–55.

30. *DWW*, 124–25; *OBH*, 169, 175; Polanyi, *Personal Knowledge*, 322.

31. *DWW*, 125.

32. *DWW*, 125; Polanyi, *The Tacit Dimension*, 4; cf. Clark, *Divine Revelation and Human Practice*, 111.

33. *DWW*, 140–41.

34. *DWW*, 128.

relationship.[35] His conclusion is stark and gripping: "This much I have learned: a self-concept which cannot be reflected through the perspective of another self (not just any self—but a self 'relationship') without being altered, cannot be held as real."[36] This is not a shallow and superficial view of "community" that simply involves church pot-luck dinners and sharing slogans, but a community that may involve separation, the kind of community that Dietrich Bonhoeffer had in prison through letters with his friend Eberhard Bethge. Anderson knows that this will be challenging: "And will they understand my joy or interpret it as betrayal? They will understand, for I know how to love—even in separation."[37] Anderson wrote this when he resigned from his pastorate in Covina, California after ten years to go and pursue his Ph.D. Community is not to be separated from ministry.

Doubt is not just an intellectual problem but it leads us to the core of relationship: love. "Love dares to include doubt as the first principle of faith. . . . But love does not fear doubt, for it springs not from reason but from reality. The unreasonable circumstances provide only the first stage of doubt, let doubt go beyond, says love, doubt love if it dares!"[38] This includes the reality of suffering. "God comes to Us in the reality of our frustration and does not force us to deny that which is real to affirm that which is merely true."[39] How much evangelical piety easily rationalizes suffering, seeking for a divine "reason" or "plan" and ends up denying its reality in the lives of the sufferer. This rationalization is not what the incarnation is about, yet there is an enriching in God that comes to us in the suffering. "We may never laugh again without a tear, but we will love again. And not with love that moves with desperate anxiety—with compulsive need, but love enriched with suffering," for we have been taught by the One who learned obedience through suffering.[40]

There is no idealism or romanticism in Anderson's relational theology. "Love is essentially tragic. Who dares to love must be prepared to

---

35. *SOG*, 35–37; *SP*, 2–4.
36. *SOG*, 38–39.
37. *SP*, 93–94.
38. *SOG*, 50; cf. *SP*, 72.
39. *SP*, 76.
40. *SP*, 77–78.

embrace the tragic for the sake of holding fast that which is loved."[41] This recognizes that love will not always live easily with the moral society. "The essence of the tragic is a collision between two or more values in real life where no single answer is the right one. The moral issues in life are layered and complex. Choices sometimes have to be made, and failure to act due to moral uncertainty may itself constitute betrayal of the human bond that unites us."[42] What does it truly mean to be compassionate? "The compassionate person is prepared to enter into the arena of the tragic for the sake of upholding human life in situations where the simple good is not possible. The moralist avoids the tragic by taking a stand for moral principle as having priority over real life choices."[43]

Relationship does not end with ministry, so that "ministry" is only church committees and planning sessions but the really dreaded moment of actually daring to preach the Word of God. Is the Word of God only "printed characters upon expensive paper" or "ancient monograms hallowed in their ambiguity by the reverence of centuries? Or does God speak again?"[44] This is an existential wrestling for the preacher that one cannot and should not avoid. "The only profile of my ministry is the dimension of reality and truth in my own life."[45] This is not a matter of making Jesus "relevant," but it is a matter of Jesus being present, a real presence. "Does Jesus move among us with disarming glance and searching heart? Does He care about overdue bills, interminable pressures, painful memories, strained marriages? Yes, of course, but then how does He speak? These words are not precise enough to be discovered in the Scripture."[46] Anderson at one time easily accepted preaching with "its unapproachable fascination," but now realizes that "the possibility of preaching lies in its necessity, not in its duty."[47] "I have never entered the pulpit but that my heart burned. . . . This does not make it any easier to face the crises—only more difficult to turn away."[48] The necessity for preaching is in nothing less than the real presence of Christ in the midst of our fallen humanity.

41. *DWW*, 141.
42. *DWW*, 141–42.
43. *DWW*, 142.
44. *SOG*, 39.
45. *SP*, 81.
46. *SOG*, 40.
47. *SOG*, 40.
48. *SOG*, 40.

Ministry as Real Presence

The Lord's Supper as Doing Evangelism and Sustaining Personhood

For Anderson, if the community participates in the continuing real presence of Jesus Christ, then the implications of this for the practical and even moral life, not just the sacramental, of the church are staggering, if not risky. Community is not simply a place of "holiness" but also of "wholeness;" not one without the other, if it is the community of the risen Lord.[49] Exclusion of the poor at the Lord's Table in the Corinthian church and Paul's admonitions to them (1 Cor 11:17–30) have often been cause for the church to emphasize the "holiness" of the sacrament, effectively restricting it to professing Christians. If the church participates in the ongoing ministry of Jesus Christ, how can it then exclude those to whom Jesus sat at table to eat and drink, including "tax collectors and sinners," risking great scandal (Mark 2:15)? Indeed at the Last Supper, did not Jesus knowingly give the cup and the wine to Judas himself, saying, "The one who has dipped his hand into the bowl with me will betray me" (Matt 26:23)? "Those who make an ethical value out of religion gain this value by excluding those who don't count. This is what confounded the Pharisees in what Jesus did: he enacted the reality of the kingdom of God. He did this not by mere teaching, for that would have been a platitude, but liturgically. That is, he made his own life an event which included rather than excluded."[50] Paul's argument that the believing wife "sanctifies" the nonbelieving husband and the children (2 Cor 6:14) is an argument from the incarnation, Anderson suggests. "The point is that the liturgical life by which the community enacts its life as the body of Christ reaches into the life of its members so as to include all who participate, both directly and indirectly." (This will be significant when we consider in chapter five Anderson's doctrine of the "kenotic community," the community Jesus created before the church!)[51]

This might be startling to suggest that the sacrament should be offered to the nonbeliever (although there is precedence even in John Wesley's theology of the Lord's Supper as a "converting ordinance").[52] Whatever

---

49. OBH, "Community as a Paradigm of Wholeness," 184–86, and "Community as a Paradigm of Holiness," 186–91.

50. OBH, 187.

51. HTRG, 227–38, reprinted in TFM, 302–14.

52. Wesley, *The Journal of the Rev. John Wesley*, Vol. 2, June 27 and June 28, 1740;

Paul is saying in the Corinthian passage he is certainly not addressing the prohibition of non-Christians as those who are "unworthy" to partake of the real presence of Christ.[53] Yet, Anderson is constantly challenging us to go beyond tradition to thinking according to the "inner logic" of the incarnation. And, in this way, he also bridges the often superficial gap between worship and evangelism. There is one ministry of Jesus Christ. Christian "ministries" only exist as samples of the one ministry of Jesus Christ, because, as we shall see, the church has no ministry of its own.

Community life is not to be separated from sacramental life. The problem in Corinth is "not a deviation from correct polity or the use of unauthorized liturgical forms. The problem is a breakdown in the structure of community itself."[54] "For when the time comes to eat, each of you goes ahead with your own supper, and one goes hungry and another becomes drunk. . . . What should I say to you? Should I commend you? In this matter I do not commend you" (1 Cor 11:21–22). This is the "unworthy manner" of participation (1 Cor 11:27) for which there can be grave consequences, not excluding nonbelievers. Paul at least "assumes some correlation between liturgical event and personal and physical health—in this case a negative one. By enacting a ritual that effectively destroys the bond of common fellowship in Christ at the personal and social level, they are destroying themselves."[55] Why should one be so afraid of the nonbeliever partaking of the Supper? Paul's warning was addressed to believers. "And why should the presence of sinners destroy the value of the event—unless the value of the event comes by virtue of what it excludes, in which case it is typically Pharisaical. While this practice may seem shocking to evangelical Christians, Anderson is trying to argue out of nothing less than the "inner logic" of the incarnation. Perhaps our traditional theology is not incarnational enough! Is evangelical theology willing to be self-critical enough in order to allow traditional practices to be criticized or are evangelicals just as uncritically bound to tradition as those other Christian fellowships they might criticize? In this, as in many

---

Bowmer, *The Sacrament of the Lord's Supper in Early Methodism*, 107. See the caveat by Geoffrey Wainwright in "Letters to the Editor," 2.

53. See the discussion in Berkouwer, "Unworthy Partakers" in *The Sacraments*, 244–58.

54. *OBH*, 185.

55. *OBH*, 185.

other aspects of his theology, Anderson presents a stark challenge for the future of evangelical theology.

In fact, one might extend Anderson's thinking one step further and wonder pastorally about those who are struggling with doubt. Should one partake of the Lord's Supper if one is struggling with faith, if one is doubting? What is it that will resolve doubt, however, but the real presence of Jesus Christ? In fact the argument might be strongly made that in times of doubt and struggle there is no place that is more important for one to be than in the presence of the Lord, sitting with him at his table, partaking in his body and blood.[56] This is not "a magical, one-for-one correlation that endows a liturgical event with the power to kill. I am, however, suggesting a general correlation between wholeness of the body and the rituals by which the body enacts its own life together," in contrast to the "demonic liturgy" that Paul warns the Corinthians against (1 Cor 10:21).[57]

Anderson again has not left theological anthropology behind, for liturgy and sacrament are to be expressions of the community that promotes personhood.

> Community as a liturgical paradigm of personhood has the power to restore wholeness to persons where there has been disintegration and fragmentation. This is the community in which Christ is present and active through the activity of the members. It is the place where there is no 'other end of the table' where I am permitted to defy love through indifference and anger or to crave love in silent despair and hunger. Such community is the place where my aloneness is exorcised and my wholeness is enacted. It is the place where I leave more of a total person than when I entered.[58]

This is a fantastic quote in which Anderson demolishes the dualism that is often sustained separating community, personhood, and worship. Practically speaking, if the liturgy does not address my loneliness, then something is wrong, something is theologically wrong at the heart of our Christology: Is Christ present or not? Zwinglians, take note! Yet sacramentalists need to heed Anderson's words that to be "liturgical" need not leave out the spontaneous and free expression of joy: "There is authentic liturgical community when we are eating together with discernment and

---

56. See Kettler, *The God Who Believes*, 56.
57. *OBH*, 185.
58. *OBH*, 186.

love, open to each other's humanity. It is when we are laughing together with freedom and without guile and rancor, when like children we actually have moments of play."[59] Again, belonging is the essence of being human. What implication does that have for the Lord's Supper? "The original condition is that of belonging. Our true origin as God brings us into being is not that of separateness and isolation, but that of belonging and being partakers of his covenant love. We do not first become believers, as those who have yet to find true value, and then belong in order to count. Rather, we are included by God before we include ourselves."[60] Belonging, in other words, matters first, before belief. This sounds very risky, however, to American evangelicalism, but only because its theology has often been inconsistently christological, and more based on the conversion experience of the individual believer. The result has often been dehumanizing forms of evangelism. "Too often, evangelism takes place outside the event of community, where there are no rituals of reinforcement and no context of belonging. When conversion to Christ is understood first of all as a private and individual decision, incorporation into the community of Christ will become more of a religious or ethical duty. Now that you have been saved, the person is told, you *ought* to join a church."[61] Genuine ritual, including the Lord's Supper but not restricted to it, reinforces authentic personhood, a personhood of belonging that reflects the belonging of the Son to the Father in the Spirit, the triune God.

"Does Jesus Think About Things Today?": The Real Presence of Christ in All of Ministry

Ray Anderson challenges theology and the church to reclaim and rethink the "real presence" of Christ. Not to be restricted to often-outdated Protestant vs. Catholic squabbles concerning the Lord's Supper, Anderson dares to bring a theology of the real presence of Christ into every area of the ministry of the church. This even includes hermeneutics, how we interpret the Scriptures in the context of ministry. Thus, in a chapter in the volume *The Shape of Practical Theology*, "The Resurrection of Jesus as Hermeneutical Criterion," he provocatively asks, "Is Jesus not only the

---

59. *OBH*, 186.
60. *OBH*, 189.
61. *OBH*, 189.

Ministry as Real Presence

author of inspired Scripture but, as the resurrected and living Lord of the church, also a contemporary reader and interpreter of Scripture?"[62] Or, as Anderson puts it in the wonderfully titled essay, "Does Jesus Think About Things Today?" in the volume *Dancing With Wolves While Feeding the Sheep*, "If the body of Jesus was raised, and his brain also, then do you think that Jesus has ever had a new idea or thought concerning God's purpose for the past two millennia?" or "Do you think that he is just sitting at the right hand of the Father leaving us with the Bible and the words he spoke to us before he ascended to heaven without having anything new to say?"[63] To ask, "What would Jesus do?," indeed, assumes his absence![64]

These questions for many evangelical believers will immediately raise some ready red flags! Is Anderson questioning the sufficient authority of biblical revelation and the "finished" work of Christ, and even the sufficiency of God's foreknowledge to know his "plan" for humanity and the cosmos? If Jesus thinks "new" thoughts today is that just a guise to bring in whatever novelty that liberal theology wants that might accommodate to the prevailing culture, so that the church can be "relevant" to modern and postmodern culture? Does Anderson here betray that, in his heart, he is a liberal theologian?

These questions are understandable. Yet the basis for Anderson's agenda here is to boldly push the envelope of the heart of the faith: the resurrection of Jesus, and therefore the reality that he is, indeed, a "real presence" in the church and its ministry, not just restricted to the Lord's Supper. If one embraces a real presence theology, Anderson contends, one must be ready for its profound implications that maybe the church has not really taken seriously enough until now.

This may be true for the perplexing and often divisive issue of hermeneutics. How should the church read the Bible today? Simply look for the author's original intention, like an archeological dig?[65] Is hermeneutics simply coming to grips with our obvious biases and prejudices that modern and postmodern critics have acknowledged shape every community's interpretation of Scripture? This is no academic problem exclusively, of course, as issues of women's ordination and homosexuality are often cited

62. *SPT*, 77.
63. *DWW*, 35.
64. *ETEC*, 136.
65. See Watson, "Hermeneutics." In *The Cambridge Companion to Christian Doctrine*, 76; *ETEC*, 123.

as case studies in pastoral hermeneutics that create widely divergent responses. So Anderson's thesis is suggestive: "The resurrection of Jesus to be the living Lord of the church constitutes a continuing hermeneutical criterion for the church's understanding of itself as under the authority of Scripture."[66] Hermeneutics likes to acknowledge that there are "two horizons" that need to be reconciled: the horizon of the original biblical authors and the horizon of the contemporary world.[67] The result is that often the contemporary horizon becomes an abstract concept of values or ethics, a principle of "love" or "justice," for example, that is simply a kind of lowest common denominator but which does not do right by either the robust concerns of the original biblical authors or the concrete questions of the contemporary scene. As an alternative, Anderson argues for taking the real presence of Christ seriously, in deed as well as in word: "As the criterion for both the original and contemporary meaning of the text, the Lord himself sustains these two points in a creative and positive tension. In this way the horizon of the original occasion of the text and the horizon of the contemporary interpreter are not really fused at all but remain quite distinct. Paul is permitted to say what he said as the command of the Lord in his pastoral hermeneutic, without forcing the text to be read in a way alien to the original context."[68]

This is particularly relevant to the ordination of women, which Anderson sees as the movement of the Spirit of God to bring new gifts to the church.[69] In an autobiographical comment about the history of Fuller Theological Seminary, he observes that exegetical gymnastics were required to recognize that, yes, indeed, women should be eligible for the Master of Divinity degree because the faculty "did not view the work of the Holy Spirit in anointing these women for ordained pastoral ministry as a text to be read alongside of their reading of the biblical text."[70] "The Word of God" must be interpreted by "the Work of God." "Both are gospel narratives and each interprets the other. The Holy Spirit is the bond be-

---

66. *SPT*, 79.

67. See Thiselton, *The Two Horizons*, and chapter 6, "It's About the Work of God, Not Just the Word of God" in *ETEC*, 117–37.

68. *SPT*, 88.

69. *ETEC*, 128–34; cf. "The Praxis of the Spirit for the Liberation of Ministry" in *SOM*, 117–28.

70. *ETEC*, 129.

tween them."[71] This is not true, he believes, with embracing homosexuality. The difference is the "biblical antecedent." Whereas there are biblical examples of women leaders in the Old Testament, the same antecedent cannot be said for approving of homosexuality. For Paul in the midst of the conflict over circumcising the Gentiles finds a biblical antecedent in his view that this was not to be required in Abraham, who was reckoned righteous before he was circumcised (Rom 4).[72] This is God's "eschatological preference," the work of the Holy Spirit, the presence of Christ that comes out of the future, not just bound by the past.[73] There is no such biblical antecedent for homosexuality with the foundational understanding that human sexuality is bound up with the image of God (Gen 1:27).[74]

There are several emphases at the heart of considering the resurrection of Jesus in the church in a hermeneutical sense, including questions of apostleship, salvation, and the rule of faith, but most intriguing, it seems to me, is the eschatological sense.[75] This is what I would call "the eschatology of humility" in Anderson's thought, as signified by the importance of a passage in Paul's first letter to the Corinthians that Anderson often cites: In Paul's defense of his authority before the critical Corinthians he appeals to eschatology: "But with me it is a very small thing that I should be judged by you or by any human court. I do not even judge myself. I am not aware of anything against myself, but I am not thereby acquitted. It is the Lord who judges me. Therefore do not pronounce judgment before the time, before the Lord comes, who will bring to light the things now hidden in darkness and will disclose the purposes of the heart. Then each one will receive commendation from God" (1 Cor 4:3–5).

The judge of hermeneutics will finally be God, and that in the eschaton, not by a human court, or even judging oneself.[76] Therefore, a humility is called for, in which we are justified by faith alone, living in the mercy of God, even as we read Holy Scripture. This is true in the life of the New Testament church itself. Did they not have to wrestle with accepting the reality of the risen Lord in their midst, and therefore wrestle with the

---

71. *ETEC*, 119.
72. *ETEC*, 125–26.
73. *ETEC*, 125–28.
74. *SOM*, 126–28.
75. *SPT*, 79–86.
76. *SPT*, 85.

text of the Old Testament, particularly the place of Israel and the Law? Was not this the distinction in the book of Acts between the church of Jerusalem that clung to historical precedent and the "emerging" church of Antioch that boldly embraced Gentiles into the church?[77] In fact, can the words of ancient Scripture really continue to speak to us as the Word of God and not just be sources of ancient religion if this is not the case?[78]

Anderson is not unaware of the dangers here. But is this simply a slide into subjectivism, so that everyone sees in Scripture what they want to see? Anderson's answer is subtle but important. "When we ask, 'Are there any absolutes?' we can answer, 'only what *is* absolute!'"[79] This is a question of avoiding idolatry, in other words. Is our confidence really in our tradition, our spirituality, or our reason, or really trust in God? "Our concepts and principles formulated by abstraction from what exists in a created world are surely not more absolute than the world itself!"[80] The place of the particular, and again, the particular human person, is important here for Anderson. When Jesus heals on the Sabbath and says, "The Sabbath was made for humankind, not humankind for the Sabbath" (Mark 2:27), he is establishing the concrete, needy individual as the absolute that God gives, not just an abstract moral regulation, as the Pharisees did.[81] "Jesus did not claim to break or destroy the law of Moses but to fulfill it in accordance with God's purpose for the restoration of broken and estranged humanity (the "biblical antecedent" for Jesus) (Matt 5:17; Luke 24:44)."[82] Anderson argues for the same theological anthropology in his approach to divorce and remarriage, as we have seen in chapter three.[83] The problem is when the Law is only interpreted as a text and set asunder from the work of God. "Those who only knew the Sabbath as a law perceived only the surface of the word of God now revealed in the work of God. The saying of Jesus thus became a new text of the Word of God, but only as a result of the narrative text of the work of God."[84] This

77. *SPT*, 86. This is the major theme of *ETEC*.
78. See the argument underlying the whole of Childs, *Biblical Theology of the Old and New Testaments*.
79. *SOM*, 20.
80. *SOM*, 20.
81. *SOM*, 20.
82. *ETEC*, 121.
83. *ETEC*, 132–33.
84. *ETEC*, 121.

is not to mean that there is a superiority of the narrative text of the Work of God. "When both Word and work are lighted by the Spirit, one (the Word) from behind and the other (the work) from the future, both come alive as revelation."[85]

What is significant here to realize is that "ministry" is not just how we apply "biblical principles" to practical situations, but is the actual continuing ministry of the risen Lord Jesus. Simply trying to get back to the author's intended meaning of Scripture is not enough. (Ray Anderson and his friend on the Fuller faculty, Daniel Fuller, had a lively debate on this for years.) "This approach, while attempting to extract truthful content from the Scripture text, does not really get to the depth of the Word of God as living Word with a contemporary voice, but merely extends the surface of the text backward as a conceptual act—for there is no way actually to recover the historical moment in which the text emerged."[86]

The Rampaging Holy Spirit in a Human Place— "Housebroken" by the Humanity of Christ

One should not sacrifice genuine, real humanity and personhood on the altar of religion. This is a constant theme in Ray Anderson's theology of ministry, and ministry as theology. This becomes particularly acute when one considers the doctrine of the Holy Spirit, for where does religion have such a potential for an insidious presence than in talk about the Spirit? Yet is the absence of the Holy Spirit often an indication that a theology has forsaken the real presence of Christ? What alternative would a theology of the real presence of Christ in ministry mean for the significance of the Holy Spirit? For Anderson, the real presence of Christ is integrally connected with the doctrine of the Holy Spirit, and *vice versa*: his doctrine of the Holy Spirit is integrally connected with the real presence of Christ.

Often neglected is the relationship between the Spirit and the humanity of Christ, and therefore, our humanity. Yet in the baptism of Jesus we see that the beginning of Jesus' ministry is the Holy Spirit (Matt 3:16–17). Anderson remarks, "I believe that this is significant. It is only when Jesus is filled with the Spirit at his baptism that his life and ministry

---

85. *ETEC*, 123.
86. *ETEC*, 124.

become evident as a manifestation of the work of God."[87] Anderson is fond of quoting the second-century theologian Irenaeus, who sees the rampaging Spirit of God in the Old Testament becoming "accustomed" to humanity through the humanity of Christ, even a "domestication" of the Spirit.[88] Students of Anderson's lectures will remember that he would often add, with a mischievous twinkle in his eye, that we can even say that the Holy Spirit was "housebroken" by the humanity of Christ![89]

What would bring Anderson to use such a thought like "housebroken"? Only because we need to be shocked into thinking how imperative it is for the humanity of Christ to harness sheer deity, the God that we cannot control, although we try. This is crucial so that our humanity would share in the power of the Spirit, yet still remain our genuine humanity. "It is Christ who is our mediator and intercessor with the Father. Thus, from a practical standpoint as well, the Holy Spirit unites our own humanity with Christ so that we do not fall back on our human weakness in prayer and worship but rather, empowered by the Spirit of Christ from within, our own spirit is permitted to be fully human without confusion and distortion."[90] Anderson is thinking here of Romans 8:26: "Likewise the Spirit helps us in our weakness; for we do not know how to pray as we ought, but that very Spirit intercedes with sighs too deep for words." Anderson's concern for personhood is never far behind in his thought. Our personhood is not obliterated but sustained by the Holy Spirit as the real presence of Christ within and among us. This is only done if the Spirit is not to be separated from Christ. "Anyone who does not have the Spirit of Christ does not belong to him. But if Christ is in you, though the body is dead because of sin, the Spirit is life because of righteousness" (Rom 8:9–10). Otherwise, we are only confronted by sheer, ineffable deity, deity that is disconnected from our humanity. This is what has happened, Anderson contends, in some manifestations of the charismatic movement. Anderson's view is cogent: "In my judgment, there are some theological inadequacies with the attempt to ground God's power in the Spirit alone. Viewing humanity as only an instrumental vehicle for the Spirit

---

87. *SOG*, 128–29.
88. Irenaeus, *Against Heresies*, 3.17. Cited in *SOG*, 129.
89. *SOG*, 129.
90. *SOG*, 130.

does not provide for the effect of the Spirit on humanity itself."[91] What is at stake is both the humanity of Christ and our personhood. "Humanity is in need of more than its physical or even emotional healing. The power of spiritual renewal is found in the actual humanity of Jesus Christ as the bearer of the very life of the Son as divine logos, not merely as a human instrument though which God displayed his divine power."[92] Evangelism, therefore, must not be practiced without respecting the real humanity of real people. The christological foundation for this is in the vicarious humanity of Christ, "by which his priestly ministry includes all who are suffering in their own humanity."[93] "When we consider that Jesus was filled with the Holy Spirit 'without measure,' we see that this experience did not make him less human but more human."[94] In contrast to viewing the manifestation of the Spirit as "super" human or "spiritual," a christocentric theology of the Holy Spirit sees the Spirit as creating the very human, and very social, fruit of the Spirit (Gal 5:16–26).[95] "The Holy Spirit adds no content to our spiritual life other than that of Jesus Christ."[96]

If the fruit of the Spirit creates social manifestations such as love and peace, then instead of speaking of the Spirit as only creating manifestations within the individual, the work of the Spirit must be seen as an environment, an "ecological" theology of the Spirit, if you will.[97] Quoting Wesley Carr, saying, "The Spirit becomes for the believing community more the environment in which it lives than an object of its consciousness," Anderson pronounces, "I wish that I could write that on the wall of every church!"[98] Grafitti is very common in southern California, where Anderson lives, but what brings him to be so passionate about this statement? He contrasts two kinds of churches.[99] One is the wax museum, "where the living and dead mingle cautiously and circumspectly, so as not to disturb each other. When the church appears to lack spiritual vigor and vitality, a new infusion of the Spirit may be necessary—someone

---

91. *SOG*, 132.
92. *SOG*, 132–33.
93. *SOG*, 133.
94. *ETEC*, 174.
95. *ETEC*, 165, 174; *SOG*, 134.
96. *SOG*, 134.
97. *ETEC*, 164.
98. *SOM*, 134; *ETEC*, 159.
99. *SOM*, 134.

who knows how to do spiritual CPR!"[100] The other are churches that "are so preoccupied with the Spirit that environmental chaos and confusion reigns." What follows is a perversion of the use of spiritual gifts. Ministry is that which precedes the use of the gifts.[101] This is different than a church that finds its identity in either "a hierarchy of leadership" or "a common polity."[102] "The Spirit does not create offices but rather ministries."[103] Anderson concludes boldly, "I have come to the conclusion that an individual is not given a gift of the Spirit because he or she needs it but because the community of the Spirit needs that individual."[104] So perhaps ministry is not just playing a permanent "role" in the church but becoming used to the Spirit in ways that might seem very unexpected to us.

What is at stake ultimately is the adventure of ministry and whether or not it will be the ministry of Jesus Christ. "I know that my own spirit is too tame when it should be adventurous. My spirit can be too impulsive and sometimes brash, when it should be measured and modest. My spirit can waver in doubt and uncertainty when I should be brave and bold. This is why I ask for the Holy Spirit to come alongside of my spirit, not to take my place but to make my place more resemble a home where Jesus lives than a college dormitory."[105]

The real presence of Christ, through the Holy Spirit, has become "accustomed" to our humanity as well, making a "home." A theology of real presence has to possess a sense of home. A theology that does not give a sense of "coming home" is not worthy of being called Christian theology. Jesus is in the business of building homes for those who are homeless. "And if I go and prepare a place for you, I will come again and will take you to myself, so that where I am, there you may be also" (John 14:3). This is a theology that is truly humanizing, not just demonstrating religious power. "I don't want the Spirit of God to wake me up in the middle of the night when I need my rest. I don't want the Spirit of God to make me anxious in order to seek first the kingdom of God. I don't want the Spirit of God to make me bark like a dog or laugh like a hyena in order to fulfill

---

100. *ETEC*, 159.
101. *SOM*, 134.
102. *ETEC*, 169.
103. *ETEC*, 171.
104. *ETEC*, 176.
105. *SOG*, 134.

a craving for 'more of God.'"¹⁰⁶ The contrast with this is a place that feels like home, a very human place. This is what it means to be filled with the Spirit.¹⁰⁷ "I have calmed and quieted my soul, like a weaned child with its mother; my soul is like a weaned child that is within me" (Ps 131:2–3). The Spirit may find us restless, but rest is the goal, a very human rest.

Ministry as the Real Presence of Christ

"All ministry is God's ministry."¹⁰⁸ Again, Anderson's essay, "A Theology for Ministry" in *Theological Foundations for Ministry* is seminal. If this is true, as we have seen, ministry is that which precedes and creates theology. This is also true of the church, if the church is to participate in the on-going ministry of Jesus Christ. This ministry is a ministry of "real presence" because it is first of all, not just trying to meet the "needs" of the world, but the ministry of the Son to the Father that in turn receives direction in ministry to the world. "All ministry is Christ's ministry of faithfulness to the Father on behalf of the world."¹⁰⁹ "Incarnational ministry" is not the youth ministry trying to "hook" the popular kids in high school in order to attract the others! This is hardly what Jesus did in picking the twelve. Incarnational ministry, rather, is relational because it is a reflection of the relationship between the Father and the Son in the Spirit. "Christ's primary ministry is to the Father for the sake of the world, not to the world for the sake of the Father. This means that the world does not set the agenda for ministry, but the Father, who loves the world and seeks its good, sets this agenda."¹¹⁰ Without the Trinity, incarnational ministry is just a cheap slogan for trying to be "relevant," and in turn quickly becomes a manifestation of what T. F. Torrance called the contemporary church's "built-in obsolescence."¹¹¹ What Torrance said in 1975 is unfortunately all too relevant today, when the church seeks "with the aid of all available media to make the Gospel understandable

---

106. *SOG*, 135.
107. *ETEC*, 162.
108. *TFM*, 7; *SOM*, 5.
109. *TFM*, 20.
110. *TFM*, 8.

111. T. F. Torrance, "The Church in the New Era of Scientific and Cosmological Change" in *Theology in Reconciliation*, 272.

within the mental habits or current thought-forms which people already have, and thus to eliminate as far as possible any gap between the Gospel and the paradigmatic mould of contemporary society."[112] That has happened in the church because of our negligible attention to the doctrines of the incarnation and the Trinity. Anderson is suggesting a way forward in terms of ministry that is both incarnational and trinitarian, not one without the other. Otherwise the current rage for trinitarian theology can only be another language for romantic speaking about "relationship" and "community," nothing different than liberal theology and the social gospel have promulgated for years.

"Ministry cannot be construed solely as the practical application (or technique) which makes theological knowledge relevant and effective."[113] As we have seen that this is true for theology, this is also true for the nature of the church. "To say that all ministry is God's ministry is to suggest that ministry precedes and determines the Church."[114] We must say this because of our Christology, if our Christology truly includes the ministry of Christ, that which belongs to him. "The on-going ministry of Jesus Christ gives both content and direction to the Church in its ministry. Jesus is the minister *par excellence*. He ministers to the Father for the sake of the world, taking the things of God and disclosing them faithfully to sinners, and taking sinners to himself and binding them graciously into his own Sonship to the Father."[115]

Practically speaking, the real presence of Christ is both sacramental and relational even in proclamation. Building upon Karl Barth, Anderson stresses that the real presence of Christ means that preaching has already occurred.[116] "For those who take the incarnation seriously, proclamation has already occurred in the Word made flesh. All subsequent proclamation has its possibility based on this actuality."[117] The burden of, or even the possibility of, preaching lies heavy on the shoulder of every preacher. What do we preach? Why do we preach? How do we have the gall to preach? But ministry as the real presence of Christ does not leave preaching up to us. The incarnation itself is God's "sermon," God's word. Anderson

---

112. T. F. Torrance, *Theology in Reconciliation*, 272.
113. *TFM*, 7.
114. *TFM*, 7–8.
115. *TFM*, 8.
116. Barth, *Church Dogmatics*, IV/1, 227.
117. *TFM*, 19.

fleshes out Barth's insights in terms of viewing ministry as first of all God's ministry. And the only way we know God's ministry is through Christ's ministry. Ministry, therefore, is not what "we do," our part of the contract with God. Again, God is on both sides of revelation and reconciliation.[118] Do we have any part in preaching, then? Of course, if we believe in the place of the Holy Spirit in ministry and in our lives as enabling us to participate in the on-going ministry and life of Jesus Christ.

"Every act of ministry reveals something of God."[119] This powerful statement of Anderson's has the potential to unleash a torrent of practical, hands on thinking concerning the ministry of the church. This brings us back to the doctrine of God. In fact, it is a sign of the poverty of ministry practice today when we are not consciously examining our concepts of God and how it affects what we do in ministry and how we do it. From our attitudes towards divorce and remarriage to whether or not children should partake of communion, to the question of baptizing a stillborn infant, a theology is at work; the questions are, What kind of theology? and What kind of God?[120] Therefore, ministry can be different than what we thought. "Ministry is much more than the teaching of biblical concepts and the application of pastoral skills in accordance with approved rules and guidelines."[121]

A Case Study to Consider:
"'For the Son of Man Has No Place to Lay His Head': Seeing Christ in the Homeless and Destitute"[122]

Facts and Dilemma

In Russ' (not his real name) sophomore year at the University of Kansas, he was leading an evangelistic group Bible discussion. For this Bible discussion, he and his fellow Christians would evangelize in the Lawrence, Kansas community, inviting those whom they met to sit in with their

---

118. *TFM*, 11.
119. *SOM*, 7.
120. *SOM*, 7–9.
121. *SOM*, 9.

122. This case study was provided by Randy Myers, a graduate student in ministry at Friends University.

discussion of pertinent biblical topics. One evening, prior to the Bible discussion, Russ led a small contingent of this evangelistic group out on Massachusetts Ave. in Lawrence, looking for people to invite to their upcoming discussion. As they were inviting people, a disheveled, older, dirty-looking man approached them, asking if he could attend the discussion. Not wanting to shun the man and wanting to show the love of Christ, Russ said he could. Even though the discussion group primarily reached out to college-aged students, Russ figured this man could use the company and the rich spiritual conversation of the discussion. Thus, the small group and this man hopped into a car for the discussion group. Along the way, this man found Russ' onyx and gold ring very interesting and tried to take it off his finger. Needless to say, Russ was quite perplexed and concerned about his and others' safety. After a few words, the man quit trying to remove the ring and they arrived for the meeting. During the discussion time, this man sat very quiet and observant, never speaking.

After the discussion, the man seemed a bit subdued. He seemed to be genuinely touched by God's Word and wanted to talk more about his life, in light of the discussion. He also mentioned that he was extremely hungry, having not eaten anything substantial for a few days. Russ decided to take him to his apartment and feed him dinner. So he prepared a meal of fried chicken, mashed potatoes, green beans, and biscuits. The man ate voraciously at dinner. Only after he was finished did he begin speaking of his life. He was a Vietnam war veteran, living under a bridge for a couple of years and could not seem to put his life together. He desperately desired to do so, but after a series of attempts, had given up hope of ever truly changing his life. He was an alcoholic and had been a little drunk when he came across the evangelistic group, thus his clumsy attempt at removing Russ' ring. He asked if he could stay the night with Russ in his apartment, for he had not slept in a bed for a while, but Russ said no. He offered to pick him up every evening at 6 pm at the bridge and they could continue their conversation. Russ then took him back to the bridge.

The following day Russ went to the spot to pick him up but he was nowhere to be found. Russ looked for quite some time, even encountering a few other homeless folks under the bridge but could not find the man. After this failure in finding him, Russ felt a strange, paradoxical guilt. On the one hand, he felt that he had done his best in serving him, giving him his heart and showing the love of Christ, and yet, he felt he could have done more and neglected to do so.

Ministry as Real Presence

Did Russ do all that he could or could he have done more?

Questions to Ponder

What are the implications of these thoughts from Anderson's theology of ministry?

1. "Hospitality is a greater miracle than teaching, for in it truth becomes actualized so as to effect new dimensions of personhood."

2. Sacramental acts are based on Jesus as the *leitourgos* (minister). "He is the liturgist, who chooses the fields, the shops, and the streets as his sanctuary in which to render service to God." Jesus continues to do "rituals of reinforcement" through the church.

3. "Community is more than a social event. It is the re-enactment of the personhood of Christ himself (his body), and the manifestation of his own service *(latreia)*. This ongoing ministry of Christ through his humanity continues through the human community as his body."

4. All of life is sacramental, therefore all caregiving can be said to be spiritual. "It is in this sense that I suggest we view all authentic human caregiving as essentially spiritual (whether or not ostensibly religious) and that the *care* given by the caregiver be considered a *sacrament* in a secular (not primarily religious) sense."

5. Does Russ put himself in the homeless man's place, like when Anderson speaks of the dying man, Colin? How is that the ministry of Christ?

6. "Far too often, in our attempts to be priests, we end up only being clowns. Holiness occurs in the street, not always in the temple. Wherever humanity finds itself, no matter how tattered and torn, no matter how lost and forlorn, is where liturgical acts should take place. For here there is vulnerability, here it counts." Did Russ perform any "liturgical acts" for the homeless man?

7. "The human spirit is the core of the self as desiring, cherishing, longing, and believing. . . . To share our spirit is to receive the other into the sacred shrine of what is most personal and dear; to share the spirit of the other is to be welcomed freely and trustingly into their holy of holies."

8. "Love is essentially tragic. Who dares to love must be prepared to embrace the tragic for the sake of holding fast that which is loved." Is the tragic a part of Russ' frustration in his limited ability to help the homeless man?

9. "The Word of God" must be interpreted by "the Work of God." "Both are gospel narratives and each interprets the other. The Holy Spirit is the bond between them."

10. "The Spirit becomes for the believing community more the environment in which it lives than an object of its consciousness."

5

MINISTRY AND MISSION

Community as Kenotic and Ek-static

The Kenotic Community: God Emptying Himself into Solidarity with Humanity

ONE OF RAY ANDERSON'S most enduring contributions to theology is in ecclesiology, with his theologies of *the kenotic community* and *the ek-static community*. These are the climatic themes in Anderson's seminal work on incarnational theology, *Historical Transcendence and the Reality of God* (1975) (selections are reprinted in the volume edited by Anderson, *Theological Foundations for Ministry*). The kenotic community, first of all, is not the same as the church, the community of the disciples of Jesus. Yet, it is the first community that Jesus created: sitting at table with sinners and publicans (Mark 2:15). This was the graphic portrayal of what the Fourth Gospel dramatically begins as the act of the incarnation: "the Word became flesh and lived among us" (John 1:14).

Anderson has not left the importance of the real presence of Christ, but merely included it in consideration with that vexing issue of the nature of Christian mission: How is Jesus Christ in the world today, and what is our participation in it? "What is the form of Christ in the world?" the question Dietrich Bonhoeffer asked from prison in the middle of Nazi

Germany.[1] If one begins with the incarnation of God in Jesus Christ, then one should not possess a Presence without a Form, unless one becomes victim to Docetism, that ancient church heresy that denies that Jesus was human for the sake of protecting his deity (1 John 4:2). Even within the New Testament church this apparently became an issue among those who interpret Paul and justification by faith as a way to excuse one from good works. So the Epistle of James is very clear that faith without works is dead, particularly if one refuses to clothe an ill-clad brother or sister or deny food to one in need (Jas 2:15–16; 2:26). "To speak then of Presence without also speaking of form is to lose touch with reality."[2] "The Reality of God" seen in the incarnation is the reality of God's love and therefore it cannot exist without a form. "Disembodied love is a state of mind, and thus does not exist at all."[3]

Presence exists with Form because of the incarnation, which is the "historical" disclosure of God's otherness, his "transcendence," thus, what Anderson calls "historical transcendence." For God to be God in the world involves presence and form together, Anderson will argue in *Historical Transcendence and the Reality of God*, a stimulating contribution to the doctrines of God and Christology, as we have seen. "Therefore, and on this point hangs the argument of this book, the transcendence of God is a reality of Spirit in which the historical existence of the man in whom the Spirit dwells is re-formed according to the form of Jesus Christ, the Incarnate Word, who is at once the image of the invisible God and the image in which man is created."[4] So Christian existence can even be called "lived transcendence," Anderson dares to say.[5] What he proposes is to reconcile the chasm between the doctrine of God and the doctrine of the church, two doctrines that have historically rarely spoken to one another! To do so, however, Christology has to flow from ecclesiology; there must be Presence with Form.

Therefore, how is the church to stand before the world if the church participates in the kenotic community? Anderson is blunt: "If there are

---

1. Bonhoeffer, *Letters and Papers from Prison*, 279–80.
2. *HTRG*, 227.
3. *HTRG*, 228.
4. *HTRG*, 229.
5. *HTRG*, 294–305.

two sides to humanity, Christ will be found on the wrong side."[6] If the church is joined to the kenotic community then it should not arbitrarily separate itself from the disreputable of the world in order to protect its reputation and even existence. In doing this it only follows its Lord. "He was not a religious man in the way that men think of the religious 'side of life.' He did not have access into the privileged sanctuaries of the priests. In the midst of a religious culture that prized appearance and cultivated form, he appeared among men clothed simply in grace and truth."[7] Building upon Karl Barth's critique of religion, Anderson sees the solidarity in the incarnation as challenged by religion when "the essential solidarity between God and man is obscured in the religious movement which originates in man himself."[8] This has a penetrating critique even of the *visibility* of the church before the world. "The kenotic community does not merely penetrate the world as a privileged community which maintains its own distinctive boundaries and identity—a form of 'spiritual colonialism'—but the penetration can only be one which bears the 'incognito' of the Incarnation itself."[9]

The practical challenge here for Anderson, of course, will be the question of whether the church, by participating in the kenotic community, will in effect be sowing the seeds of its own destruction as it is more and more influenced by the "sinners" and the "publicans" in the kenotic community. How can the church keep its identity when it is in solidarity with the world? is a perennial question throughout church history. One thing the church must not do is break the "incognito" "by setting the sacred over against the secular and supernatural over against the natural. This would itself be a conforming to the world rather than conforming to the Incarnate Son of God."[10] We have seen both this refusal to separate the sacred and the secular and his critique of religion in Anderson's plea for a "pre-theoretical" approach to the human person that acknowledges the spiritual nature of the human but does not equate the spiritual with the religious.[11] Often the question is put in term of the "boundaries" or

6. *HTRG*, 252.

7. *HTRG*, 252.

8. *HTRG*, 253. Cf. Barth, "The Revelation of God as the Abolition of Religion," *Church Dogmatics*, I/2, 280–361.

9. *HTRG*, 254.

10. *HTRG*, 255.

11 See *SCSS* and Anderson, "Toward a Holistic Psychology."

"marks" of the church (such as preaching of the word and the celebration of the sacrament).[12] Anderson suggests that a more incarnational approach is to begin with Christ's solidarity with all of humanity and then understand the church as proceeding out from that group. "The kenotic community, considered incarnationally, is the foundation of all human community, and the church can never deny its common participation in this community without denying Christ himself. This, of course, does not yet say what 'church' is, but it says what 'church' cannot be—namely, an entity which distinguishes itself from the world by breaking solidarity with humanity."[13] To be "evangelical" and "incarnational" is not to break faith with solidarity. "The reason for this is that *both* the boundary and the centre, both the solidarity and the difference, are rooted in the transcendence of God as historically given in the life of Jesus Christ."[14]

There are implications for spiritual formation here as well. For Anderson has a trenchant criticism of what he calls "the kenotic way of life."[15] The kenotic community should not be confused with those who live the kenotic way of life, the way of the religious in every age. "What is even more dangerous is that the assumption of a kenotic way of life on the part of the church in the world occludes the very truth which the *kenosis* discloses, and envelopes the ego of the church ever more securely in a posture of humility."[16] The kenotic way of life is insidious in its stance of humility before the world, as it was for the Pharisees and Sadducees of Jesus' day, and thus incurring his rebuke (Matt 23). "A life which is devoted to self-emptying can be a life committed most powerfully to a manner of self-existence."[17] These are words that desperately need to be heard in our age in which "spiritual formation" and "spiritual disciplines" have rightly received new emphasis in the church, but with the danger of perceiving spirituality as devoting one to a life of "self-emptying," ostensibly following the model of Jesus (Phil 2:5–11), yet perhaps ending up in a life of self-centeredness. At this point Anderson is critical of Bonhoeffer when he speaks of the church as only being for "others": "The church is

---

12. On "boundaries" see *HTRG*, 268ff.
13. *HTRG*, 259
14. *HTRG*, 270.
15. *HTRG*, 229.
16. *HTRG*, 229.
17. *HTRG*, 229–30.

Ministry and Mission

the church only when it exists for others."[18] In this way, the danger of spiritual formation is also the danger of mission as a whole in the church, whether it is evangelism, missions, or social ministry, the danger of the kenotic way of life. What appears at first to be "radical," Anderson points out, is really "superficial."[19] The church could conceivably give away all of its earthly possessions to the poor and feel quite "humble." Yet in doing so it would immediately cease to exist in order to continue to participate in the ministry of Jesus Christ. Unlike the rich young ruler, it would not be obeying the concrete command of Christ, a point that Bonhoeffer elsewhere stresses quite strongly.[20] This would not be "living in the Spirit" but by law and duty and not from the transcendence of God in Jesus Christ.

At the heart of the kenotic community is the one *kenosis,* or "emptying" of God in Jesus Christ, the one who "emptied himself, taking the form of a slave, being born in human likeness" (Phil 2:7). This is a revelation of the trinitarian life of God. "When we probe the depths of *kenosis* . . . we discover that what appears as a way of life through self-emptying on the part of the man Jesus, and thus looks to an observer like a God giving away his divinity, is actually a quality of life intrinsic to the relation of Father and Son which is exemplified by the Son's human obedience even unto death."[21] The incarnation and the cross make this possible in the midst of real, not ideal humanity. "From the furthest side of human estrangement, the intra-divine transcendence exposed itself as a community of love which overcame the estrangement and reclaimed the estranged ones by inclusion in the divine life itself."[22] Anderson is careful to draw a distinction here between actuality and mythology. For this he draws upon the vicarious humanity of Christ, "the man who is for God." "Historical transcendence, then, is not simply a divine act playing on the stage of historical existence, such as would be commonly expressed in mythological language, but it is the God who is for man also acting as the man who is for God."[23] There is no purely forensic atonement here, extrinsic to the being and love of God. Neither is the place of the Holy Spirit

---

18. Bonhoeffer, *Letters and Papers from Prison*, 382–83.
19. HTRG, 230.
20. Bonhoeffer, *Ethics*, 388ff.
21. HTRG, 231–32.
22. HTRG, 232.
23. HTRG, 280.

to be ignored. "The Holy Spirit, who was 'being accustomed' to dwelling in human flesh, as Irenaeus puts it, through the intimate union of the Son with humanity, becomes one with the kenotic *form* as explicated by the Son in his humanity and thus creates a kenotic community which is itself an image or likeness of the intra-divine community."[24] This community is not necessarily a community of believers. The publicans and sinners were not believers when Jesus sat down with them and at that moment created a "community." "When the Holy Spirit assumes the historical existence of the other man as the form of Christ for me, a cripple is no less real than a whole person."[25] And I think that "cripple" can be understood as crippled spiritually, emotionally, or morally, as well as physically.

The implications of this are staggering for the attitude of the church towards the world. *The first community of Jesus is not the church but the kenotic community.* It is out of that kenotic community that the church is called forth. Yet the church must never forget that it continues to be a part of the kenotic community, in solidarity with others.

Anderson refuses to restrict the exhibition of the transcendence of God to only delivering revelation, particularly only in the form of the Scriptures. There are "two marks of visibility" of the transcendence of God: one, in the historical revelation of God in Christ and the Scriptures, and two, in "the presence of the Spirit in the concrete life of the other person in the community, or one could say, in the concrete existence of the community itself."[26] Anderson later views these twin poles in terms of both the Work of God as well as the Word of God, both of which are necessary for revelation and in "the resurrection of Jesus to be the living Lord of the church constitutes a continuing hermeneutical criterion for the church's understanding of itself as under the authority of Scripture."[27]

It is at the point of mission, however, that the kenotic community has its most profound implications. Since this is the first community that Jesus created, before he called any to "follow me," it can be said that there are no qualifications or conditions to be in this community. "It seems clear from the character of kenotic community as it has been exposed, that a conversion 'experience' cannot be demanded as the qualifying act

---

24. *HTRG*, 232.
25. *HTRG*, 234.
26. *HTRG*, 235–36.
27. *ETEC*, 117–37 and *SPT*, 90.

on the part of a person for his belonging to the kenotic community."[28] What would this mean for mission? Would not this mean that the missionary enterprise of the church has as its first step to represent a kenotic community in which, yes, there is a real presence of Jesus Christ, but without first demanding a call to conversion.

For the past several years, the Church of the Savior, an independent evangelical church in Wichita, Kansas, has the worked with the Legacy ministry, a Christian arts outreach started as memorial to the Christian musician Rich Mullins. Drawing mostly upon teenagers that the court put under the care of the Salvation Army, the congregation has organized an intensive week of serious, and fun, sessions on the whole range of the arts. Not just used as a gimmick in order to "give them the gospel," this ministry has provided the beginning of relationships that have continued throughout the year as a team would regularly meet with the boys and the girls. I would suggest that what is being demonstrated here is what many Christian ministries realize: the first creation by Jesus Christ is the kenotic community, in which men and women, boys and girls, see demonstrated the "emptying" of Jesus' love upon them without conditions or qualifications. Out of this community then come those who respond to the call to follow Christ; but not without first being exposed to the kenotic community. Anderson adds the important caveat: "But it must also immediately be said that participation in the kenotic community does involve receiving as well as being received. And it may well be that only after 'being received' for a considerable length of love (one would naturally say 'time,' but these 'lengths' have a duration which only love can measure!) can a person muster the strength and the will to receive."[29] The goal of the kenotic community does not leave behind Anderson's obsession with theological anthropology, an *actual* growth into the reality of their own personhood, which is the capacity to live in love."[30] Mission should not become "disembodied" from God's desire to respect and grow our personhood. "The kenotic community can be said then to be the 'home of personhood' where man is both received as a person and then, at the same time, receives his personhood."[31] And all this before "conversion"!

28. HTRG, 236.
29. HTRG, 236.
30. HTRG, 236.
31. HTRG, 237.

For some, this can be very puzzling, challenging and upsetting, if one sees grace as beginning with our movement of faith. Anderson's genuinely evangelical theology of the incarnation does not have that problem, an insurmountable problem, perhaps, for much of traditional evangelical theology and mission. Yet, how does one argue against Anderson biblically, according to the Jesus of the gospels? He is the one who "emptied" himself. Is the church willing to follow him in that?

> For the kenotic community, poverty is not that which it gives away, but that which it receives; powerlessness is not in the abandonment of a place in the world, but in refusing to let go of the weak for the sake of the strong; humility is not in taking less than the world, but in receiving more than the world can give. The kenotic community has no Presence other than its own existence, or rather, God's presence to himself in its existence. It has no sacristy to be profaned, no temple to be destroyed, no Prince to be exiled—or ignored.... For *such as it is*, it is the transcendence of God. The answer is in the wind.[32]

The Ek-static Community: The Movement of Community in God and Among Humanity

Ray Anderson is not content, however, to leave with a community that is only in solidarity with humanity. That may be the temptation for many contemporary ecclesiologies, which end up limiting the incarnation to an event of "solidarity" with humanity. This is the characteristic of a church that can only present social ministry, a church as only a social service agency, as well as the "contemporary" church desperately trying to be relevant in order to "communicate" to the culture. The result is that the church can only represent the agendas of the contemporary; a view of atonement that possesses representation but not substitution, a problem that T. F. Torrance clearly sees.[33] In the life of Jesus there was also an "ek-static" movement, a reflection of his trinitarian relationship to the Father, very much the basis of the vicarious humanity of Christ and of the worship by the church (if the church cares to have a theology of worship!). The bridge between the last chapter on the sacramental and liturgical reality of the

---

32. *HTRG*, 238.
33. Torrance, *Space, Time and Resurrection*, 116.

church and this chapter is obvious and is worthy of much consideration. How often is worship divorced from mission! That Anderson takes worship and mission together and further integrates them with theological anthropology is only indicative of the depth and promise of his thought.

Anderson borrows the concept of the "ek-static" from the noted Eastern Orthodox theologian, John Zizioulas.[34] In fact, Anderson may well have been the first theologian in the English-speaking world to recognize Zizioulas' ground-breaking studies in theological anthropology and ecclesiology, studies that have lead to much discussion ecumenically, throughout the church and in contemporary theology.

Anderson is concerned that the "domesticization" of the Spirit by the humanity of Christ does not make the Spirit "housebound."[35] The place of the Holy Spirit is to create "lived transcendence," not an escape from the transcendence of God. "The kenotic community is earth-related, for it exists in the same flesh as that of Jesus of Nazareth, but it is not earth-bound, for it lives in the same Spirit as did Jesus."[36] At the heart of the ability not to be "earth-bound" is the intimate relationship of the Son with the Father, in which he "stands out" (the Greek *ek-stasis*, from which we get our word *ecstasy*) in order to pray to the Father. Anderson is not far from the vicarious humanity of Christ at this point. "When we explored the kenotic life which Jesus lived, we saw that the deepest penetration of humanity and from the furthest side of human estrangement, he lived in unbroken communion with the Father. His prayers were considered as evidences of this extra-human relation on the part of a genuinely human person."[37] This "movement of communion," as Zizioulas speaks of *ek-stasis*, is in the trinitarian being of God, with very different implications for theological anthropology, in opposition to human beings as simply "substances."[38]

---

34. Originally published in the *Scottish Journal of Theology* 28, no. 5 (1975), 401–47 as "Humanity Capacity and Human Incapacity: a Theological Exploration of Personhood," this is now available as chapter six in *Communion and Otherness*, 206–49. Anderson refers to "Human Capacity and Human Incapacity" as an "unpublished essay" from 1972 in a footnote a page long in *HTRG*, 240, n.29 and Zizioulas' teaching on "presence-in-absence" on 304, n.74.

35. *HTRG*, 238.

36. *HTRG*, 239.

37. *HTRG*, 239.

38. *HTRG*, 239–40, 240 n. 29.

Preferring to speak of the ek-static community rather than the *charismatic* community, Anderson seeks to orient the church in relationship to God. "The ek-static community is a community united in one Spirit and thus participates in the life of God."[39] This is in contrast to a community that merely represents introverted humanity. "The introverted community of man seeks distinctiveness in its autonomy over and against nature, and, as a result, either worships nature, or, as is more typical of our technological age, exploits it in the name of creativity."[40] The contemporary interest in a theology of creation and ecology makes Anderson's burden very relevant. "If the church is to link up again with creation, and ecology is only one aspect of creation, the Spirit which has been so largely introverted in terms of both worship and ministry must become truly ek-static in the widest possible sense."[41]

"The widest possible sense" of the ek-static community is important because of the church's tendency to view the ek-static, the movement of worship, as purely introverted, as Anderson even criticizes Bonhoeffer for in his doctrine of worship as the "secret discipline" of the church.[42] This creates an untenable dualism with Bonhoeffer's "religionless Christianity." "One lives in the world as if there is no God, and in the cultus as if there is no world!"[43] The church comes out of these two communities, the kenotic community and the ek-static community. "Because Word and Spirit can never be separated, the kenotic community is at the same time the ek-static community. Which is to say, the ek-static community reveals to the community of man its *incapacity* which it can only experience as a capacity for community."[44] The influence of Zizioulas is obvious here. So also are the implications for a robust ecclesiology in mission, an ecclesiology based on grace (incapacity).[45] One might add to Anderson that "Word and Spirit" may be seen to correspond to the double-movement of the incarnation, from God to humans and from humans to God, the second

---

39. *HTRG*, 242.
40. *HTRG*, 243.
41. *HTRG*, 245.
42. *HTRG*, 245.
43. *HTRG*, 245.
44. *HTRG*, 250.
45. *HTRG*, 250.

being the movement of the vicarious humanity of Christ, Jesus being the man led by the Spirit (Luke 4:1).

Christopraxis: Jesus Christ and His Continuing Ministry as an Alternative to Theory Before Practice

At the heart of Ray Anderson's theology of ministry and mission is the belief that genuine ministry and mission is that which Jesus Christ is continuing. Postmodern thought has been persuasive to many in pointing out the problem of ministry as a process of beginning with "theory" which then ends with "practice." So the articulation and exposition of theology and doctrine in the church is seen as the necessary first step; then that doctrine is "applied" to a ministry situation. This reveals a reflection of a now outdated modern, Enlightenment age way of thinking that postmodern culture finds irrelevant. So much of contemporary theology, often spurred by liberation theology, advocates the importance of a theology of *praxis*.

But cannot *praxis* become simply another form of a liberal theology that begins with experience; religious, political, or existential? If ministry and mission are participating in the continuing ministry of Jesus Christ, Ray Anderson suggests that perhaps it would be better to speak of *Christopraxis*. This is continuing the line of thought that gives birth to the kenotic community and the ek-static community as reflecting the incarnation of God in Jesus Christ, God's "historical transcendence." The ministry of Jesus Christ includes both theory and practice because doctrine and ministry are inseparable, so it is much better to speak of the continuing life of Christ as its center, that is, to speak of Christopraxis. "Praxis is reflective because it is action that not only seeks to achieve particular ends but also reflects on the means and the ends of such action in order to assess the validity of both in the light of its guiding vision."[46] Establishing pristine doctrine or crafting immaculate skills in ministry could each be done and still not be the ministry of Jesus Christ. The ends never justified the means for Jesus. Eternal salvation was never achieved apart from a humane act of compassion. "Praxis, then, reveals theology in a very tangible form. In this sense, *actions are themselves theological* and as such are open

---

46. SPT, 47.

to theological reflection and critique."⁴⁷ Outcomes and effects become just as much a part of the action, rather than simply results of the action. "The production of a sermon manuscript and the mere verbalization of its content does not constitute praxis, for praxis necessarily involves the realization of an intended result or effect. The homiletics professor in seminary might award an A grade to the sermon manuscript, but from the standpoint of the purpose of the Word of God, the sermon has not realized its *telos* until the Word of God has had an effect (Isa 55:11). Praxis includes the effect of the Word as well as a presentation of it."⁴⁸

It may well be asked of Anderson, however, How is this *Christo*praxis? What distinctive does Jesus Christ bring to ministry and mission that is more than looking for the effectiveness of its actions, a principle that the Church Growth movement has made for years, and not without controversy? Anderson appeals to Jesus healing on the Sabbath (John 9; Mark 2:27) as an example of doctrine that is not abstracted from concern for humanity because "the truth of the Sabbath was to be found in the restoration of humanity, not in keeping the law of Sabbath."⁴⁹ Again the work of God must be seen in conjunction with the Word of God. "This is what is meant by praxis. The work of God in our midst discloses to us the Word of God, even as the Word of God reveals its truth in producing God's work. God's Word of truth reaches its *telos* in healing, making whole, and restoring God's created purpose. This is the praxis of God's Word as truth."⁵⁰ Ignoring this action is to ignore the work of the Holy Spirit, which does not simply "apply" the teachings of Scripture, but integrates them in the real presence of Christ. Again, the real presence of Christ, which he is continuing in his ministry in the world today, means that the ministry of the church is contingent upon God. "Christopraxis, as I have attempted to present it, upholds the full authority and objectivity of the divine Word was written in holy Scripture but only because Scripture itself is contingent on the being of God as given to us through the incarnate Word."⁵¹ Anderson adds, "Christopraxis, I have argued, is the normative and authoritative grounding of all theological reflection in the divine act

---

47. *SPT*, 48.
48. *SPT*, 50.
49. *SPT*, 51.
50. *SPT*, 51.
51. *SPT*, 53.

Ministry and Mission

of God consummated in Jesus Christ and continued through the power and presence of the Holy Spirit in the body of Christ."[52]

Anderson presents Peter and Cornelius in the Book of Acts as a concrete case study of Christopraxis in action.[53] Peter responds with protest to his vision that commands him to eat what had been unclean (Acts 10:14–15). The Spirit of God is at work although not without Peter processing it through the "theological precedence" in Scripture (Amos 9:11–12 cited by Peter in Acts 15:16–17), after Peter meets Gentile Cornelius, whom Peter now sees as "clean" through "theological discernment" based on his vision (Acts 10:28). "This theological discernment led Peter to theological innovation, and he baptized Cornelius, which is theological praxis!"[54] Subsequently, the Holy Spirit falls on the Gentiles (Acts 10:44–48). Christopraxis is at work when Peter acknowledges, "If then God gave them the same gift he gave us when we believed in the Lord Jesus Christ, who was I that I could hinder God?" (Acts 11:17). Christopraxis leaves room for theological innovation to take place, for the Holy Spirit to do something new, yet the "theological precedence" in Scripture reminds us that theological innovation is not the same as novelty, simply a capitulation to the cultural winds of change.

In terms of the ecology of the Christian community, Christopraxis is concerned not just with doing things "right," morally or doctrinally, but with particular, actual human beings. Again, we see the importance of real, not just ideal, human beings for Anderson's theological anthropology and how that theological anthropology has implications for the entirety of his theology. The ministry of the church would not be a participation in the continuing ministry of Jesus Christ if this were otherwise. And the actual human beings are ministered to in a context of a community of reconciliation and hope. This makes Christian ministry distinct.

> A social worker or psychiatrist may be able to "make" people better or to "make" the conditions of human existence better. But the end result tends to be just that—a result, a product that the "maker" can detach himself or herself with no consequent loss of identity or meaning. However, in Christopraxis the act itself becomes the embodiment of a life of community and wholeness that is derived from God himself through Christ. Thus we know that

---

52. *SPT*, 53.
53. *SOM*, 28–31.
54. *SOM*, 30.

> reconciliation is more than making people or conditions better; it is inextricably involved with revealing the power and presence of God through the act.[55]

In contrast, beginning with theory and then ending in practice detaches the minster and the theologian from actual people in ministry and therefore becomes dehumanizing. "In the same way, we can also say that there are forms of ministry that purport to proclaim revealed truths of God and to indoctrinate disciples in those truths, but if they do not also touch broken and alienated human lives with liberating and healing power, they are not of God."[56] In all of this, Christ remains alive and present so that there should be no detachment of the minster and the theologian from Christ. "In this way, it can be said that Jesus is not only the subject of proclamation (the one about whom we preach), but he is himself the proclaimer in every act of proclamation (the one who proclaims himself through the event of preaching)."[57]

Ministry, therefore, is not based on merely doctrinal articulation or the honing of communication or relational skills but on *discernment, integration,* and *credibility*.[58] Discernment perceives that there are not many "ministries" each of which ministers to one aspect of our humanity but one ministry of Jesus that addresses the whole person. This only happens in the midst of ministry, including the wedding of the exegetical and the practical, not in the luxury of abstract detachment. "An exegetical or hermeneutical decision regarding a scriptural teaching that is not also a judgment on behalf of the saving and gracious purpose of Scripture has not yet entered into the sphere of Christopraxis."[59] Integration promotes the connection between the work of God and the word of God so that the living Christ continues to minister among us in word and deed. Credibility becomes an imperative of one participating in the actual ministry of Jesus Christ, and in fear and trembling, commits oneself to nothing less than the judgment of God (1 Cor 4:3–4), and in doing so, experiences the freedom of not having to judge oneself or be heckled and handicapped by the judgment of others. "Christopraxis, therefore, demands a particular kind

---

55. *SPT*, 54.
56. *SPT*, 54–55.
57. *SPT*, 56.
58. *SPT*, 57. Cf. Anderson, "Christopraxis."
59. *SPT*, 57.

of competence that manifests in being credible as a presentation of Christ himself, not merely as an infallible interpreter of Christ."[60] Real presence, indeed!

Mission Before Ministry

The world is the context for the first community that Jesus Christ creates: the kenotic community. Therefore, it makes sense to Ray Anderson that mission is that which precedes and creates the church.[61] "The church exists in the center of the continuum between gospel and mission as the body and presence of Christ. The apostolic mandate is to move from the gospel through church to mission."[62] Anderson wants to avoid an equation of the church with the gospel and the mission, but will he be able to do that if he maintains elsewhere, as we have seen, an ecclesiology of the real presence of Christ? Is the church then simply a means to an end for Anderson?

Anderson sees in the church of Antioch in the book of Acts a stark contrast with the church of Jerusalem. "The Holy Spirit in the emerging church at Antioch was experienced not only as a Spirit that created ministry but as a Spirit with a mission, 'Set apart for me Barnabas and Saul for the work to which I have called them' (Acts 13:2)."[63] The church of Antioch, the church that sent out Paul on his mission to the Gentiles, was a church of mission. Anderson finds a great deal of harmony here between the missional nature of Antioch and the "emerging church" movement today.[64] One can argue for a priority of mission over ministry, but not the exclusion of ministry from mission.

> Both issue from and are directed by the Spirit of Christ, but there is a priority of one over the other. Mission without ministry can lead to imperialism. Ministry without mission can become narcissism. Ministry keeps mission from grandiosity, triumphalism and kingdom-building. Ministry keeps mission close to humanity, even if it means building a hospital rather than a temple. But mission keeps ministry from becoming a mirror in which the church,

---

60. *SPT*, 59.
61. *SOM*, 158–61.
62. *SOM*, 160.
63. *ETEC*, 181–82.
64. *ETEC*, 181.

like the mythical Narcissus, sees its own reflection and ends up withering away until it becomes a potted plant—a narcissus![65]

A critical question may be asked at this point. Can a priority of mission before ministry hold up, however, if ministry is the continuing ministry of Jesus Christ and a reflection of the eternal being of God as service, "ministry" (the Son serving the Father)? Can one speak of an eternal mission in God? Yet Anderson is quick to cite how mission and ministry need one another. Certainly the church suffers and has suffered when it does not live its ministry in the context of mission. "The church at Jerusalem was strong on ministry but weak on mission."[66] Anderson's kenotic and ek-static communities, emptying themselves into the world, and being movements of community, certainly provide a missional imperative that criticizes a "narcissistic" tendency in ministry. But does he have a trinitarian basis on which to speak of the priority of mission before ministry?

A Pentecostal, Not Just Incarnational, Ministry

A question was once raised to Ray Anderson by a pastor in Fuller Seminary's Doctor of Ministry program, a program Anderson gave theological leadership to for many years: "Is Pentecost only an experience and evangelical only a theology?"[67] By this he was questioning a self-described "evangelical" seminary that was accepting those with a Pentecostal experience but did not seem to be interested in a theology that was informed by the Holy Spirit, a Pentecostal theology. Anderson agreed. This is seen in the history of the church. "The development of an official ecclesial theology along the lines of a continuity with the incarnation led gradually to the theological and institutional marginalization of a pentecostal experience . . . the phenomena of ecstatic experience, miracles of healing and dramatic "power encounters" with demonic spirits."[68] And this affected theological education. "The traditional separation of biblical studies, church history, theology and ministry (practical theology) into separate academic divisions follows too closely the modern university model. It tends to reinforce the separation of theological study from the task of

65. *ETEC*, 182.
66. *ETEC*, 182.
67. *MOTF*, 151.
68. *MOTF*, 201.

ministry and lends support to the idea that ministry, or practical theology, is primarily a matter of acquiring pastoral, pedagogical, homiletical, or liturgical skills and techniques."[69] A "praxis-based curriculum," in contrast, Anderson suggests, would be dynamically connected to effectiveness and outcomes in ministry. Anderson wrote in 1993, "In my seventeen years of teaching in a theological seminary I have yet to experience a debriefing by the theological faculty in which those who are attempting to carry out the teaching and strategy received in school return to discuss the effectiveness of this theology with their teachers."[70] I remember Anderson relating that in his Theology of Ministry tutorial for Doctor of Ministry students he often found students who had been "inoculated" against theology because of the type of and method of theology they had been taught in seminary, primarily divorcing theology from ministry and ministry from theology!

More than just theological education, an incarnational ministry informed by Pentecost manifests the real presence of Christ today. An incarnational ministry and theology is essential for Anderson, as we have seen. "A world without Jesus but with the Spirit would be one filled with power but not with presence."[71] Yet a Christology not informed by Pentecost practically restricts Jesus to the first century. "Pentecostal experience without incarnational theology is like a sailboat with neither oars nor rudder—it can only move when there is a wind, though it cannot steer when it is moving. Incarnational theology without pentecostal experience is like a barge of coal anchored to shore. It has fuel but no fire, and even if it should burn it has no engine so as to turn water into steam and steam into power."[72]

What is needed is "a new look at Christ through the glow of Pentecost and a new look at Pentecost through the glory of the risen and present Christ."[73] What has often happened even in churches with a strong theology of the incarnation is that the incarnation becomes a museum relic, disconnected from mission and ministry today. "It is my belief that Pentecost is more than a mere historical and instrumental link between a

---

69. *MOTF*, 206.

70. *MOTF*, 205; see "Epilogue: Memo to Theological Educators," 197–209; cf. *SPT*, 317–28.

71. *MOTF*, 21.

72. *MOTF*, 25.

73. *MOTF*, 22.

theology of the Incarnation and a theology of the institutional church."[74] "Pentecost is more than the birth of the church; it is the indwelling power of the Spirit of Christ as the source of the church's life and ministry."[75] What is needed for ministry is not just equipping but empowerment.[76] "In Pentecost we see the same *ex nihilo* that lies at the core of the biblical paradigm. . . . While the disciples and early believers were followers of Jesus and witnesses to his resurrection, they were powerless until the Spirit came upon them at Pentecost."[77]

What Anderson means by "empowerment" is not just patronizing action by leaders of congregations in order to manipulate them. Instead, empowerment in a pentecostal sense meets a brutally realistic need. "Daily life has a way of disempowering people, leaving them discouraged and spiritually depressed. The church makes a mistake of offering them momentary spiritual inspiration through worship without empowering them for daily living."[78] The church may be desperately trying to help people discover their "spiritual gifts," even through "spiritual gifts inventories." "This kind of shopping for gifts as a way of mobilizing lay persons for ministry often creates initial enthusiasm and bursts of energy, but just as often can lead to personal frustration and spiritual fatigue."[79] What is needed is empowerment before equipping. "Unless empowerment precedes equipping, many people who are encouraged to exercise a spiritual gift find that their enthusiasm and motivation wanes."[80]

Our culture contributes to this feeling of lack of power. The economic downturn of 2008 and 2009 was a rude awakening for many, creating a deep sense of a lack of power over our lives. We seem to be vulnerable to both complex, impersonal economic forces as well as machinations by Wall Street barons, investment shysters, and political bosses. So much so, that early in 2009, the makers of "Tropicana" orange juice dared to change their packaging (no more "orange with a straw"). Consumers were outraged and the $35,000,000 marketing campaign went for naught as Tropicana changed back to the old packaging. One marketing com-

---

74. *MOTF*, 23.
75. *SOM*, 111.
76. "Empowerment Precedes Equipping" in *SOM*, 109–11.
77. *MOTF*, 112.
78. *SOM*, 116.
79. *ETEC*, 172.
80. *ETEC*, 172.

mentator remarked that in the present dire economic environment, this protest became a small way for many to say that they have some power over their lives! They can change Tropicana's mind by protest! Anderson's argument is that the church should first address that vulnerability and frustration through the power of Pentecost as the power of the continuing life and ministry of Jesus.

"With the resurrection of Jesus and the coming of the Spirit on the early believers at Pentecost, the earthly life of Jesus took on new significance. The *content* of the Spirit's work was understood to be a continuation of the ministry of the same Jesus who performed the works of God from his baptism to his death on the cross."[81] This brings us back to a crucial christological issue: How can we argue for a continuity between the historical Jesus and the Christ of faith?[82] For Anderson, this is not a question that should be left to the historians and their quest for "the historical Jesus." This is a theological and, indeed, pastoral and ministry issue at stake as well. Theologically, we must have the courage not to supplant but to build upon the classical christological dogmas. "I do not wish to supplant the formal dogmas of Christology," Anderson contends, "but rather to approach the historical Christ in his power as the risen Christ."[83] This is an issue that cuts deeply into our doctrine of God as Trinity and the relation between the Trinity and our Christology: "Theologically Pentecost is the beginning point for a theology of Jesus Christ because the Holy Spirit reveals to us the inner life of God as the Father of Jesus and Jesus as the Son of the Father."[84] It is only through the Spirit of God that we have access to "the mind of Christ" (1 Cor 2:10, 16).

The church is empowered by the Spirit when Christ continues his apostolic ministry, Anderson argues.[85] Apostolic ministry should not be limited to beliefs about a historically correct and consistent line from the apostles to the present day. Protestants were right to criticize their Catholic and Orthodox brethren on such an ecclesiology that equates the Spirit with historical lineage. The apostle Paul certainly had trouble with those who were suspicious of his apostolic authority (particularly in

---

81. *SOM*, 111.
82. *MOTF*, 24.
83. *MOTF*, 24.
84. *MOTF*, 24.
85. "An Apostolic Mandate" in *MOTF*, 133 and "The Church as an Apostolic Community" in *SOM*, 147–55.

Corinth) because he had not seen Jesus during his earthly ministry but was an apostle, as one who was "untimely born" (1 Cor 15:8), had "only" received from a revelation of Jesus Christ (Gal 1:12) in contrast to the "proper" way that Matthias was chosen to replace Judas on the basis of historical continuity (Acts 1:15–26).

Yet Protestants are wrong as well to practically ignore the apostolic ministry of the church. Often Protestants, like Catholics, limit apostolic foundations to origins in the first century.[86] The "Protestant principle," at least in its conservative form, is often a cry to go back to "the first century church," meaning the church of the Bible. Instead, we should speak of apostolicity because Christ is the chief apostle, "the apostle and high priest of our confession" (Heb 3:1). (There are certainly echoes of the vicarious humanity of Christ here.) The church has an apostolic and prophetic witness, however, only when Christ is the "cornerstone" (Eph 2:19–20). As he possesses an incarnational ministry and an empowering ministry, Christ the apostle also has a "transforming ministry" in which the church can dare to say along with Paul, "we have the mind of Christ" (1 Cor 2:16) as Christ uses the church to change lives.[87] "Because Christ is a living Christ and because he continues to exercise his will and authority through his Spirit, the mind of the apostle must be open to the will of Christ as revealed through the Spirit in every contemporary situation."[88] Mission involves the continuing ministry of Christ the apostle, the "sent one," the meaning of apostle. "The apostolic continuity of the church must be found in its life under the transforming power and presence of Christ rather than in its conformity to the form of the church in the first century."[89]

Anderson again brings in the importance of *praxis*, Christopraxis, not just beginning with sound theory and then "applying" it with ministry skills.[90] God is not just concerned about whether or not we do things with the right ideas or with the right skills, but with the effect on the community and the world. "There is no Christ for the world other than the Christ who is present in the form of the Holy Spirit indwelling persons and empowering them for witness and ministry."[91] The healings in the gospels and

86. *MOTF*, 21.
87. *SOM*, 152–53.
88. *MOTF*, 123–24.
89. *MOTF*, 128.
90. *MOTF*, 28.
91. *MOTF*, 44.

the book of Acts are significant because they are outcomes and effects of God working.[92] "Christopraxis is thus more than advocacy, it is a ministry of the grace of God to those who are without grace."[93] "The praxis of the Holy Spirit" is when "our preaching and teaching reaches God's purpose in the transformation of human hearts and lives."[94] The Holy Spirit works through "the structures of reality" of God's actual actions through the church in the world.[95] We often end up avoiding the praxis of the Spirit when institutions such as the church are identified with the incarnation or even the work of the Holy Spirit so that whatever the church does (or does not do) is said to be identical to what God is doing (or is not doing). "One cannot avoid the praxis of the Holy Spirit in creating a theology of the church. One cannot set aside Pentecost as marginal and resurrection as unnecessary in order to link the church directly to the concept of 'Emmanuel'—God with us in the form of the person and teaching of Christ."[96] This betrays a christological deficiency in our theology; we have in effect lessened if not denied the distinctive humanity of Christ. "Any attempt to do this tends to confuse the humanity of the church in its ideal form with the humanity of God in Christ as the real form of the church."[97] There is a great deal at stake here. "Without Pentecost as the beginning, the church can lose its connection with the mission and ministry of God. The church then becomes the incarnation of a human ideal rather than the continuing mission of the incarnate One, Jesus Christ."[98] Anderson comments how it is noteworthy that it is only with the Gospel of John, written much later than the Synoptic gospels or the letters of Paul, that we have a fully developed theology of the incarnation. "Following Pentecost and the ministry of the Spirit through the early church, a theology of the Incarnation as the source of that ministry gradually became clear. The continuity between the Spirit released at Pentecost and the historical Jesus was an essential link in that theology."[99]

---

92. *MOTF*, 44.
93. *MOTF*, 52.
94. *MOTF*, 29.
95. *MOTF*, 29.
96. *MOTF*, 34.
97. *MOTF*, 34.
98. *MOTF*, 34.
99. *MOTF*, 48.

READING RAY S. ANDERSON

God's Responsibility in Ministry . . . and Burnout

Anderson shares his own story of frustration in ministry when it appeared that despite his efforts he could never meet all the needs in the congregation. (This is poignantly laid out in the chapter entitled "Clergy Burnout as a Symptom of Theological Anemia" in *The Shape of Practical Theology*).[100] He had allowed his ministry to become identical with his calling, he reflects later.[101] The turning point for Anderson was when he began to reflect on the life and ministry of Jesus. Why did Jesus hesitate before the tomb of Lazarus (John 11)? He could have rushed to the side of Lazarus and immediately raised him from the dead, but he "stayed two days longer in the place where he was" (John 11:6). "As I reflected on this incident I began to understand that Jesus' ministry was not connected to ministry-related incidents but to his obedience and service to the Father."[102] His food was to do the Father's will (John 4:34) because he could not do anything on his own without the Father (John 5:30). Anderson is speaking here of the vicarious humanity of Christ, because he concludes that the basis for our calling is found in the calling of Jesus to be obedient to the Father, not a calling to a particular ministry.[103] "It is bad theology to have to love the world more than God, and to confuse our service to God with our being sent into the world. It is bad theology to interpret the calling of God in terms of the needs of the world, rather than in our being sent to the world to do God's work and reveal his glory."[104] The humanity of Christ does not function as just an instrument where God can either be satisfied with punishment for our sins or as an example for us, but as an actual sanctification of our humanity.[105] "The christological basis for a theology of calling into ministry rests upon the ministry of Christ as the one who provides the service *(latreia)* of love and obedience to God on behalf of the world. The humanity of Christ stands as representative of all humanity in service to God.[106] (Should Anderson also include that

---

100. "Clergy Burnout as a Symptom of Theological Anemia" in *SPT*, 284–90.
101. *MOTF*, 50.
102. *MOTF*, 51.
103. *MOTF*, 51.
104. *SPT*, 287.
105. *MOTF*, 158–59.
106. *MOTF*, 52.

Christ is the *substitute* for all humanity, as a judgment upon our senses of "calling"?)

What does it mean, in other words, to have a successful, or even "Spirit-filled" or "faithful to Christ" ministry? Anderson is blunt. "A theology that cripples and destroys the self-esteem and sense of worth of a minister is not made better by 'success' in ministry.... A healthy theology, of course, is a theology of a loving God who knows that to be God is to be responsible, even for our faltering and fallible efforts."[107]

This theology was hammered out by Anderson on the anvil of his own pastoral experience. He tells the story of the suicidal woman he counseled once, and who continued to come back with hours of demands. "There had been interminable hours of pastoral counseling recalling the promises and grace of God. But now, after midnight, the end of my resources had come.... Quietly, I stood up and said, 'I'm going home and going to sleep. I am not God and I am not anyone's savior. In the morning, if you are alive, call me and we will talk again."[108]

"If you are alive...!" Anderson knew that with the audacity of those words he would have to be ready to preach her funeral in the coming days. "For I sensed that God was now my advocate and not my adversary. Yes, I was betting on my judgment that the woman would survive—and she did. But it was a turning point for me. I understood more of the grace of God than I had ever before. I understood the grace of God because I was in a position to receive the grace of God."[109]

In his words to the suicidal woman, his ministry was depending on God's responsibility. "A healthy theology is a theology of a loving God who knows that to be God is to be responsible, even for our faltering and fallible efforts."[110] This is one of the most graphic and poignant pictures of the vicarious humanity of Christ in action of which I know. Through this experience, Anderson surprisingly felt a certain goodness about himself, surprising because are not Christians taught that we are sinners? The change was that God was acting in him, even within his limitations. "I felt called to be an agent and instrument of that good. I felt good about myself because I felt forgiven and loved. No longer was I living on the edge of

---

107. *SPT*, 287–88.
108. *SPT*, 288.
109. *SPT*, 288.
110. *SPT*, 287–88.

that terrible marginality in ministry, where the abyss always looms threateningly over and against every action."[111] In effect, this is Jesus' theology of ministry, remaining while Lazarus was sick, healing on the Sabbath, because of his faith in and obedience to the Father.[112] When Jesus prays to the Father concerning the disciples, "As you have sent me into the world, so I have sent them into the world" (John 17:18), he is not prescribing the disciples to just imitate him, but to imitate his continuing ministry that is always in harmony with his incarnate ministry, a ministry of grace, forgiveness, and healing.[113] It is good, even imperative, for those who minister to first know that for themselves.

A Case Study to Consider: "Trouble in Middle School Ministry"[114]

Facts and Dilemma

Natalie (not her real name) is a new student in Westminster Church's middle school ministry. Ross, the middle school director, was happy to include her in the group for two months when she first came on Sundays. She quickly became involved with the group in other ways, attending Wednesday night Bible study and coming with the group to other activities outside of church, the most recent was the weekend fall retreat to Westminster Woods camp. Natalie is a very intelligent girl with an engaging personality. She often demonstrates a knack for asking tough questions, many of which would never enter her peers' minds.

From this initial description one would conclude that Natalie joining the group has been smooth sailing. That, however, has not been the case a good share of the time. Natalie has had problems adjusting to the group. There are a myriad of reasons why this is the case. One such reason for why Natalie has had some difficulty adjusting is that she can be very up and down. One day she is happy and the next time she is sad. On the surface this does not seem to be a big deal, especially when considering

---

111. *SPT*, 288.

112. *SPT*, 287–89.

113. *SPT*, 289.

114. This case study was provided by Derek Maris, a graduate student in ministry at Friends University.

her stage in life, but with Natalie the moods are more extreme. If it is a good day, then she is all smiles and loud laughter. She will be very sociable and friendly. On the other hand, if she is unhappy she is quiet and withdrawn, only breaking out of it to deliver sarcastic and cutting remarks. During those times it isn't unusual for her to be in a verbal dispute with other students, usually other females. Again, many of these issues are not unique to Natalie. What sets her behavior apart from the other middle school students is the intensity of these behaviors when compared to those around her.

Part of the reason for these rather vicious mood swings lies in the perception that Natalie seems to want to be the center of attention. Her extreme moods and behaviors make this goal attainable for her. However, this need for attention hasn't gone over very well with some of her peers.

A major event in her past is driving this insatiable need for attention. When she was about eight years old, her dad divorced her mom and left the family. At this point Natalie has not seen her dad in a few years. At the fall retreat she confided to the speaker that her dad had left the family. As she was relaying this event to the speaker, she was understandably upset about communicating personal information. She had even asked why God allowed this to happen.

Natalie remarked that she had tried to connect with God before. She said she asked God to help her once and she did not feel him at all. In fact, despite all her knowledge regarding the Bible Natalie confessed that she figured she was an atheist, if anything. This admission somehow leaked to some of the students and during the retreat Natalie was the victim of some heavy-handed evangelism tactics that only angered her. It is possible that the residue of the "evangelism attack" can be found in Natalie's view that many other students "judge" her.

How would you minister to Natalie?

Questions to Ponder

What are the implications of these thoughts from Anderson for your ministry to Natalie?

1. "To speak of Presence without form is to lose touch with reality." Jesus "was not a religious man in the way that men think of the religious 'side of life.' He did not have access into the privileged sanctuaries of

the priests. In the midst of a religious culture that prized acceptance and cultivated form, he appeared among men clothed simply in grace and truth." How could the evangelistic efforts towards Natalie reflect "presence without form"?

2. "The kenotic community does not merely penetrate the world as a privileged community which maintains its own distinctive boundaries and identity—a form of 'spiritual colonialism'—but the penetration can only be one which bears the 'incognito' of the Incarnation itself." How does one respect Natalie as a member of the kenotic community?

3. "For the kenotic community, poverty is not that which it gives away, but that which it receives; powerlessness is not in the abandonment of a place in the world, but in refusing to let go of the weak for the sake of the strong. . . . The kenotic community has no Presence other than its own existence, or rather, God's presence to himself in its existence."

4. "The ek-static community is a community united in one Spirit and thus participates in the life of God." How does this contrast with the "introverted community" that confronted Natalie?

5. "Praxis, then, reveals theology in a very tangible form. In this sense, *actions are themselves theological* and as such are open to theological reflection and critique. . . . In the same way, we can also say that there are forms of ministry that purport to proclaim revealed truths of God to indoctrinate disciples in those truths, but if they do not also touch broken and alienated human lives with liberating and healing power, they are not of God. . . . Christopraxis, therefore, demands a particular kind of competence that manifests in being credible as a presentation of Christ himself, not merely as an infallible interpreter of Christ."

6. "Mission without ministry can lead to imperialism. Ministry without mission can become narcissism."

7. What is needed for ministry is not just equipping but empowerment. "In Pentecost we see the same *ex nihilo* that lies at the core of the biblical paradigm. . . . While the disciples and early believers were followers of Jesus and witnesses to his resurrection, they were powerless until the Spirit came upon them at Pentecost."

8. On accepting God's responsibility: "For I sensed that God was now my advocate and not my adversary. Yes, I was betting on my judgment that the woman would survive—and she did. But it was a turning point for me. I understood more of the grace of God than I had ever before. I understood the grace of God because I was in a position to receive the grace of God."

6

MINISTRY AS THE FUTURE OF CHRIST COMING INTO THE PRESENT

Eschatology: Toward the Church of the Final Century

It is typical of Ray Anderson that his eschatology would be wrapped up in his ecclesiology, his view of the church. The trinitarian, communal nature of God, the social meaning of being human, and his relational Christology all point to a view of the "end times" that refuses to forsake community for eschatological speculation. The church is the sign of the kingdom of God, as Anderson has stressed in his lectures on ecclesiology for years.[1] In fact, a criticism of Anderson may be that his ecclesiology eclipses much of eschatology. If this is so, however, it is not because of any connection between the church and continuing to uphold "Christendom," a church of the status quo. Anderson's church is too much of a community that simply participates in the continuing ministry of Jesus Christ. And that community is eschatological, bringing a distinctive tang to Anderson's doctrine of the church as well as to his eschatology. What appears to be an eschatological gap in Anderson's theology may be an eschatologically charged dynamic in his ecclesiology.

It was a friend's question that ignited Anderson's thoughts about the church and the end times: "I wonder what church Jesus would like to visit if he suddenly returned to earth?"[2] Our typical response might be to explore the alternatives: theologically (conservative or liberal?) or liturgi-

---

1. *ETEC*, "It's About Kingdom Living, Not Kingdom Building," 96–116.
2. *SOG*, 157.

cally (traditional or contemporary?) but that only reveals the shallowness of our thinking about the church today.

Ideals of the church are easy to come by. Anderson had a typical informal "free church" ideal in his younger days, he admits.[3] I certainly can resonate with that having come out of the "Jesus Movement" of the early seventies myself. Yet a radical and critical incarnational theology, such as represented by Karl Barth in ecclesiological debates with Emil Brunner, may cause us to stop and consider the actual church that is the body of Christ, with all of it warts, rather than to constantly dream about the ideal. "The church we see is really the church we get," Anderson concludes.[4]

The ideal church has often been conceptualized as "getting back" to the "original." The Protestant Reformation, influenced by Renaissance Humanism, certainly sought to get back to "the sources" of the faith, which the Reformers saw in the Bible. From then on, Protestants of all stripes have seen the centrality of the Bible for all theology, including ecclesiology. The ideal church is "the New Testament church," the church of the first century.

For Roman Catholics and Eastern Orthodox there is a great deal of respect for and security in the centuries old tradition and institution of the church. Anderson recognizes that attraction. "I think that I understand why more than a billion people find satisfaction and security in being attached to something so permanent and so mystically powerful as religious ritual that draws them into the *mysterium tremendum* of divine reality."[5] But the advantage of security may sacrifice the riskiness of faith. "A venerable history is far more compelling than a vulnerable future. A historical Christ (even though wrapped in tradition) is more predictable than a Christ emerging out of the future in the breath of the Spirit."[6] Traditionalists may not restrict the "true" church to the church in the first century, but their orientation is to maintain the tradition of the past in the present. But what has happened to eschatology then? And does one's Christology really reflect the eschatology of the Spirit, so that in a theology of "real presence" (important to Roman Catholic, Eastern Orthodox, . . . and Ray Anderson) is the presence of Christ today as the present of

3. *SOG*, 161.
4. *SOG*, 160.
5. *ETEC*, 200.
6. *ETEC*, 200–201.

the Christ who through the Spirit is coming from the future, that is, to make all things new? The problem for all of us—Protestant, Catholic, and Orthodox—is that we are too satisfied with a "predictable" Christ. This is the danger of all kinds of orthodoxy.

Anderson, however, does not mean to denigrate the Church Fathers and tradition here. "There is something to be said for having an anchor to the past that holds firm against the fickle and often contrary winds of the present. But anchors, like tradition, only serve to hold us in place. No sailor will raise the sails to the wind until the anchor is pulled. I would like to lift the anchor, raise the sail and test the wind of the Spirit in order to move toward that which lies ahead of us."[7]

This, according to Anderson, was the basic difference between the church of Jerusalem and the church of Antioch in the book of Acts. "Here we see that the emerging church at Antioch, which came out of the future by virtue of the Spirit of Christ gathering and baptizing both Jew and Gentile into the body of Christ, accepted, affirmed, and claimed to be part of the community of Christ at Jerusalem. The Jerusalem church did not reciprocate."[8] The "cornerstone," Anderson stresses, is Jesus Christ (Eph 2:20). Apostolic tradition is embodied in Jesus the Apostle (Heb 3:1) whose apostolic ministry was incarnate, risen, and proclaimed, and continues even today as the one who will come (Heb 13:8).[9] "As the risen and ascended Lord who is coming, Christ's apostolic authority reaches toward us into the present time as the creative power for the church's apostolic ministry in every generation."[10] There is a consistency between the incarnate and historical, the risen and proclaimed, and the present and coming Christ, yet not forgetting that Christ comes from the future doing new things.

Key for Anderson as a young pastor was Jesus' prayer to the Father, "As you have sent me into the world, so I have sent them into the world" (John 17:18). How then has Christ been sent into the world? He has been sent as the one who is coming back. The goal should not be to be the church of the first century but the church of the *final* century, when Jesus returns, the kind of church Jesus desires to find when he returns. "While

---

7. *ETEC*, 202.
8. *ETEC*, 204.
9. *ETEC*, 205–11.
10. *ETEC*, 209.

Ministry as the Future of Christ Coming into the Present

the first century of the church is normative for the revelation of Christ as the incarnation of God and the redemption of humans from sin and death, the return of the same Christ and the resurrection from the dead constitute the normative praxis of the Spirit."[11] "First century" perspectives are limited, in contrast to much of Protestant tradition. The question is how seriously we take the resurrection and ascension of Christ and the giving of the Holy Spirit. "The resurrection and ascension of Christ followed by Pentecost and the praxis of the Holy Spirit during the present age orients the church to the final century of historical life rather than merely to the first century."[12] This does not mean the neglect of ecclesiology (as among some Protestants) but its reestablishment in an eschatological mode. "My view of the church changed when I began to look at it from the perspective of the final century rather than the first."[13] So the question to us should be, What kind of church will Jesus find and should Jesus find when he returns? That is living eschatologically.

The church of the final century is, indeed, in continuity with the incarnation of the first century because he is the same Jesus Christ. So the incarnation provides the "prescription" for the church today.[14] The "manifesto" that Anderson created as a pastor in Covina meditated upon John 17:18: "As you have sent me into the world, so I have sent them into the world." Thus, as Jesus came into a formalistic religious culture, he challenged it with grace and truth, speaking one language for saint and sinner and living a lifestyle that was human not religious.[15] The test for truth in the church, therefore, is how much we reflect the character of Jesus Christ. Jesus created community and human relationships with integrity, so the church is called to do nothing less.[16] This is the church that Jesus should find waiting for him, not one obsessed with legalistic ethics, doctrinal purity, or ideological conformity. Jesus did not speak much of the church, but much about the kingdom of God, where God reigns.[17] Here is where Anderson is convincing in speaking of the dynamic relationship between the church and the kingdom of God.

11. *ETEC*, 211.
12. *ETEC*, 212.
13. *SOG*, 166.
14. *SOG*, 163
15. *SOG*, 161.
16. *SOG*, 162.
17. *SOG*, 158; *ETEC*, "It's About Kingdom Living, Not Kingdom Building," 96–116.

"In more than forty five years since taking my first seminary class I have read much of the literature on the origin, nature, and form of the church only to come to the conclusion that Jesus probably does not care as much about what the church looks like as much as what we expect from him when we look to the church for the sustenance of the Spirit in our daily life."[18] The eschatological Spirit is still at work as the church participates in what Christ and his real presence continues to do. We are back again to the humanity of Christ and our connection to him. "Christ is the prescription and the church is to be there for us to fill and renew it. I need healing when my humanity becomes ragged and rough, when I am broken and bitter, when I feel despair and depression. God assumed that humanity in the person of Jesus who, in his own human life healed the wounds and restored humanity to its completeness in the image of God."[19] This is the church that Jesus expects to find when he returns. Living this is living eschatologically.

Heaven and Hell: Criteria and Conditions?

Eschatology, particularly in evangelical theology, has always been concerned with the reality of heaven (and how to get there). That has been reflected obviously on the importance of evangelism and the necessity of a personal decision for Jesus Christ; hence, Billy Graham's magazine, *Decision*. Is it truly evangelical, however, to center theology in personal decision? Is the center of the gospel *our* faith? If so, what does that say about the grace of God and the place of Jesus Christ? Ray Anderson has wrestled with these questions, characteristically going back to Judas as a "case study" in a provocative chapter in *Dancing with Wolves While Feeding the Sheep* entitled, "Will Judas be in Heaven?"[20] In this exercise Anderson is challenging evangelical theology at its core to be truly evangelical and to question, with the help of Karl Barth, both Calvinist and Arminian determinisms. The question in the end becomes, Will evangelical theology, and particularly its eschatology, be truly *evangelical*, that is, centered in the gospel, or centered someplace else?

---

18. *SOG*, 163–64.
19. *SOG*, 167.
20. *DWW*, 49–58.

Ministry as the Future of Christ Coming into the Present

This, of course, is an extension of Anderson's queries concerning grace, forgiveness, and their extent, focusing upon Judas. A prisoner in the Los Angeles County jail had been sentenced to life for the murder of his mother and father. Knowing of Ray Anderson's book on Judas, his question to Anderson was blunt: "Can Judas really be forgiven for what he did? I did something worse than Judas, but somehow I believe that if there is hope for him there may be hope for me."[21] Anderson's response is to imagine the theological consequences of this man and his parents as a way to probe traditional evangelical theology concerning eternal destiny, but at the level of a genuine pastoral theology; something quite different perhaps from "textbook" theology.

What if the man's parents were not Christians when they were murdered? According to Calvin their destiny is determined ultimately by God. The Arminian critique locates the final criterion in the decision of whether or not one has decided for Christ before one's death. One determinism is in that of the sovereign will of God and the other is in the sovereign will of the individual. Anderson, with a little help from Karl Barth's Christology, "decides" for neither.

Anderson's pastoral heart kicks in with his theology at this point. What if this man would become a Christian, insuring his destiny in heaven? He would be going to heaven when his murdered parents would not because they have never made a decision for Christ. They would go to hell. Anderson continues, showing that he develops the keen insights of Karl Barth on this subject, insights often leading to Barth being accused of universalism. But Anderson demonstrates that this is a logical conclusion that one can have only if one accepts the premises of either Calvinism (God determines salvation) or Arminianism (human choice determines salvation). Both are deterministic and end up strangely ignoring the place of Jesus Christ in eschatology. Anderson's consistent incarnational theology paradigm will not allow that. So he follows and develops Barth's christological eschatology with a distinct pastoral and practical bent.

According to Barth, if Jesus Christ is the Elect One to both election and damnation then "God has taken upon himself the fate of eternal estrangement and so removed death as an obstacle to the possibility of redemption of all."[22] However, this does not entail universalism. It does

21. *DWW*, 49.
22. *DWW*, 55.

mean that the judgment belongs to Christ (Matt 25:31), not a purely sovereign God nor human decision. "What Barth has offered, whether or not one agrees, is a solid theological argument for the freedom of God to make a final determination of human destiny not based on a theory of predestination (Calvin) nor upon human free will (Arminius), but upon God's own act through Jesus Christ by which the power of death to determine human destiny has been once and for all overcome through the death and resurrection of God's own Son, Jesus Christ."[23]

What is left is what Anderson many times in his lectures admits to be the importance of what he calls "the doctrine of ambiguity." One can hear the loud protests to this: "At the point of where we need the most certainty, our eternal destiny, Anderson and Barth leave us with ambiguity!" Evangelical theology's most common objection to Barth—his "universalism"—demonstrates that Barth (and Anderson) are really not evangelical.

But what is more evangelical than to proclaim that God in Jesus Christ has triumphed over death so that death is not the obstacle for anyone, the murderer or the parents? Rather, something has happened to *all* humanity because the Word became flesh (echoes of Anderson's "kenotic community" have great implications here). *Grace* always occurs before *faith.* Our destiny lies in the hands of Jesus.

"Do I Have to Believe in Hell?" is another practical question that Anderson deals with in *Dancing with Wolves While Feeding the Sheep*.[24] While there is an obvious testimony about hell in Scripture, Anderson ponders the nature of "believing" about hell. Is hell in time? Is it timeless? And most of all, how does Jesus Christ relate to hell? Again, his views of "historical transcendence" call Anderson back to considering the extent of God's voluntary estrangement in the world through Jesus Christ. "How far was Jesus sent into the world?"[25] Did he go into the depths of even Judas' hell? Or is the decree of the sovereign God or the ability of our personal faith the final criteria; therefore exposing that God's love, indeed, is not covenantal but contractual? "The point is, in becoming human through Jesus Christ, God sent his Son as far from heaven as necessary in

---

23. *DWW*, 57.
24. *DWW*, 77–88.
25. *DWW*, 86.

order to provide salvation and reconciliation."[26] The question is a question concerning the incarnation and its human reality: "How far was Jesus sent into the world?"[27]

Believing in hell, therefore, is not about simply believing in an ontological entity, where our eternal destiny may be unless we make the right decision or do the right amount of good works. Rather, hell is defined by the extent of the incarnation and the atonement, Christ going to hell for us. "Hell is an extension of humanity, not something beyond what is human."[28] "If there was a hell for Jesus, there is a hell."[29] Yet Jesus was not only raised from the grave but he was raised from hell.[30]

Anderson does not embrace universalism but he does embrace Judas (and the prisoner he met) already changed by Jesus Christ when Christ sits at table with sinners, publicans, and to whomever is born witness of his grace and love. "The decisive point is in the power of the resurrection, and the reality of spiritual rebirth into the life of Christ through the Holy Spirit. All have died with Christ, but not all have been raised with Christ."[31] In the end, Jesus Christ, the one who was not afraid to "empty" himself and love the unlovely, determines who we are, even though we are the ones on the "wrong side of humanity." How then can we speak of a decision of God apart from Jesus Christ (Calvin)? How then can we speak of our ability to "decide" for Jesus as the fulcrum of salvation (Arminius)?

What Anderson adds to Barth is, ironically, the fruit of his American evangelical theology: the "new creation" of Christ, the one "born anew," therefore the possibility of a "born anew" Judas in heaven.

> So will Judas be in heaven? Not really. That is, not the Judas who is the betrayer, but possibly a "born anew" Judas through the power of the Holy Spirit in the encounter with Christ which occurs after death (2 Cor 5:10). Not the Ray Anderson who is "dead in trespasses and sins" (Eph 2:2) but a "born anew" Ray Anderson through the power of the Holy Spirit, of which I have present assurance of a future reality, the "pledge of our inheritance" (Eph 1:13–14). Both Judas and I will appear before the judgment seat

---

26. *DWW*, 86.
27. *SOM*, 102.
28. *SOM*, 101.
29. *DWW*, 85; *SOM*, 101.
30. *DWW*, 87.
31. *DWW*, 86.

of Christ. I "fear no condemnation" (Rom 8:1), and I would like to think that this fear will also be removed in the case of Judas.[32]

Evangelical theology often complains about Barth's "universalism," so Anderson has stood evangelical theology on its head: A "born again" or "born anew" experience is necessary, Anderson agrees, following evangelical theology, but not based on a sovereign God's decree or a desperate decision before death. This is not an opportunity to choose in the afterlife, as Donald Bloesch advocates.[33] Such a view still locates the fulcrum of salvation in our decision. But there is a possibility of many more (and different kinds of people!) than we might think who will be changed by Jesus meeting them, in this life or the next. As a young pastor, Anderson wrote in his journal the existential and pastoral anguish of the doctrine of hell:

> I am sorry—I simply fail to be moved with the simple statement that my neighbor is going to hell because he does not share my convictions about the theology of Jesus Christ. It is not that I am sure that he isn't, but that it seems too grotesque for words that I must put him in hell before I can love him in Christ! I do believe in hell, for myself at least. That is, I have no illusions about the reality of personal immortality and the possibility of eternal existence as a self without relationship. Perhaps that is why I cling so desperately to relationship.[34]

Anderson can never leave humanity as co-humanity far behind! His theological anthropology demands this. Moreover, his pastoral heart and theological instincts demand this.

The Terminus of Life: The Sovereign God, Human Choice, or Jesus Christ?

The pastoral heart of Ray Anderson is never better exhibited than in the chapter of *Dancing with Wolves While Tending the Sheep* entitled, "What Do I Say at the Graveside of a Suicide?"[35] The implications of the grace of Jesus Christ for eternal destiny are real and relevant for such a gut-wrenching life crisis as the one Anderson describes here. The inadequacies

32. *DWW*, 57–58.
33. *DWW*, 56–57.
34. *SOG*, 42; *SP*, 40.
35. *DWW*, 59–67.

of an eschatology based on either the sovereign God or our human choices can hardly be seen more clearly than in this situation. Is suicide the final statement that one is not of the elect? Or is it the final act of damnation, of the misuse of free will? Sadly, the church has often only had these two answers to this crisis.

In contrast, Anderson draws upon his theological anthropology that takes seriously the tragic in life. What happens when "the burden of life becomes greater than its beauty"?[36] "It is only the person who sins that shall die . . ." (Ezek 18:4). This logic of sin and death is often said to be the bedrock of our theological anthropology, not the grace of God in Jesus Christ. The result is a "bad theology" and a "bad psychology." "When this logic of cause and effect has been drummed into the mind by teachers and used by parents to frighten a child into performance acceptable enough to earn their praise, one develops a conscience rooted in fear of condemnation."[37] Shame replaces grace as the meaning of one's life.

Others quickly explain away such a tragedy: "This man placed himself outside of God's grace by taking his own life."[38] The implicit theology is clear: Human choice is the ultimate arbitrator of salvation and eternal destiny. But what has happened to Jesus Christ here? "It seems that it is not death itself, even death by one's own hand which places one outside of God's grace—if indeed this is possible! It is the intention which is the fatal sin. In this view, suicide is not only morally wrong but it is a sin against God for which there is no grace, no forgiveness, because the death removes the possibility of repentance."[39] Again, the fulcrum of salvation is seen, in this view, to be human choice, salvation by *our* repentance! How "evangelical" is this, really?

Jesus Christ relates to the death of a suicide, first of all, in the same way that he relates to all human deaths: He has taken upon our deaths and delivered us from the power of death.[40] The depths of "historical transcendence" mean that the last word about human beings is not death because that was not the last word about Jesus Christ. A sovereign God who determines that we will die and a free will determines that one can

---

36. *DWW*, 60.
37. *DWW*, 62.
38. *DWW*, 63.
39. *DWW*, 63.
40. *DWW*, 65.

take one's life are alternative views of salvation ignoring the reality of the incarnation and the cross. "Whatever caused this young man to take his own life, we do not comfort ourselves by attributing psychological grounds to place his death by his own hand, under the consequence of sin which has been removed once and for all through the resurrection of Christ. This is gospel, not grief counseling."[41] At this actual funeral service, Anderson speaks of the woman who took her life as a beautiful vase (she collected vases).[42] A vase is fragile; beautiful in appearance, but the human being in appearances can mask anxiety and terror within. This is a return to the solidarity of Christ with us that respects our fragile and tragic existences and becomes the source of our healing and hope.

Living in the Middle Zone with Christ as the Terminus

Eschatology moves us finally into the present; the present in which we have to make decisions. Anderson criticizes a theology that makes human choice as the fulcrum of salvation but he does not ignore the very real place of human responsibility in this life and before God. And this includes a responsibility even to end human life. This would disturb many. There is no appeal here to biblical proof-texts about life or arguments for "natural law." But there is Anderson's characteristic appeal to the actuality and real presence of Christ that reveals not only the actuality and real presence of God but also that of particular, real human beings. This is where we find ourselves in ethical dilemmas, not in the theology or ethics textbook. And Anderson is not afraid to see Jesus Christ in that actual, present situation. His eschatology, as we have seen, is the presence of the Christ who comes from the future, not a defender of tradition or human autonomy, what Anderson calls "middle zone" moral thinking.

"When it comes to the beginning and ending of life, we are always standing in the middle."[43] This is where we live. The past is gone; we cannot replicate it. The future is unknown (an important point for those Christians who want security for every event that will happen in the future). We live in the middle. And even eschatologically, that is where God is, the kingdom of God as "the presence of the future," in the words of

41. *DWW*, 65.
42. *DWW*, 66.
43. *DWW*, 113.

Ministry as the Future of Christ Coming into the Present

Anderson's former professor at Fuller, George Ladd.[44] Eschatology needs to be understood from the middle. This is not simply a capitulation to a status quo "realized eschatology" but an acknowledgment that the continuing ministry of Jesus Christ is ministering to the hurting right now. This Christ is the one who comes from the future.

"It would seem that we are guided toward the kind of thinking that begins with actuality and only then moves toward possibility."[45] At this point, ethics and eschatology join together in Anderson's thought. The result is "the middle zone." "To project what we know as truly 'human' backward into sheer biological material may be to think beyond what we actually know and border on the absurd. In the same way, to project what we know as truly 'human' forward into some kind of post mortal form of life can become equally absurd."[46] Working from the "middle zone" of human morality "defines and sustains human life from the center outwards, rather than from the beginning forward."[47] It might be though that Anderson breaks here with Dietrich Bonhoeffer, whose ethics (particularly on abortion and euthanasia) very much finds its basis in God as the origin and destiny of life.[48] Therefore, life should not be taken only because of human autonomy.

In another sense as well Anderson is very much in harmony with Bonhoeffer. For Bonhoeffer takes seriously (especially for his own life) the presence and direction of God in the concrete, historical moment, in Anderson's words, "the middle zone."[49] Both Bonhoeffer and Anderson want to avoid the idealism and abstraction of an ethics that ignores the real presence of Christ. Bonhoeffer is critical of an ethic that makes decisions beforehand and is not contingent upon the command of God in a concrete situation. Anderson is sensitive to this concern. So, he adds "decency" or "indecency" as moral categories to determine humanity in the "middle zone."

Anderson tells the story of the young boy critically injured in a bicycle accident. He was kept breathing on a ventilator. The father, who was a physician, said the breathing apparatus could keep him breathing

---

44. ETEC, 96.
45. DWW, 113.
46. DWW, 114.
47. Ibid.
48. Bonhoeffer, *Ethics*, 171–218.
49. Bonhoeffer, *Ethics*, 253–98.

for weeks or perhaps months. "He then asked me to consider with him the fact that this boy was already on his way to live forever with God and that we were only holding back this transition. . . . We prayed together, he performed the procedure, and then removed the ventilator, holding the struggling limbs of his son as he passed from this life to the next."[50] Anderson relates this as a place of the middle zone of responsibility and as a place where the coming Jesus Christ is present. "I realized that I was an accomplice to an act for which I had, at that time, no theological or, perhaps, ethical grounds for justification. At the same time, I felt that his was a deeply human and responsible act taken not only by a professional medical technician but by a parent."[51] There was no time to consult the theology textbooks, as Anderson remarks in his lectures. Seeking to do so, the minute you break eye contact from your counselee, they are lost. What is more important than learning correct doctrine is to learn theological *instincts*. That means never separating the humanity of Christ from his deity, and that includes his identification with our humanity. That is participating in the continuing ministry of the real presence of Jesus Christ. It is a risky, and human, business.

The Terminus of Life: Death as a Season of Hope, Not as a Struggle

Death and dying reminds us that we are creatures that share a solidarity of the sixth day with all animals.[52] We are denying our humanity if we ignore this, as much as Christians might believe in the resurrection of the dead. We are of the earth (Gen 2) as well as being made in the image of God (Gen 1). "A theology of death for human personhood must also then include the realistic aspect of death as that which belongs to one's natural life. This biological continuum of life and death, which includes a finite and mortal creaturely nature, is a limit which God established upon the human person's earthly existence."[53] What is human, however, is not determined completely by the creaturely because we are made in the image of God.[54]

50. *DWW*, 122; cf. *TDD*, 138.
51. *DWW*, 122.
52. *TDD*, 47–48; *OBH*, 22.
53. *TDD*, 49.
54. *TDD*, 48.

Ministry as the Future of Christ Coming into the Present

Hope is that which connects us to the "seasons" of life in a way that faith cannot.[55] "Faith does not have seeds, but hope does. But the seed of hope, without the faith invested in its cultivation, lies dormant."[56] This does not endorse every kind of manifestation of hope, however. "When hope is embraced where faith has not yet matured, the damage can be permanent. There is a childish hope that doesn't count."[57] Anderson tells of his father's story that on Christmas Eve the cows in the barn rise up in honor of the Christ child's birth.[58] Trying to "prove" that this was true by going out into the barn would be to miss the point of faith. "There is a certain 'murderous intention' in the need to prove or disprove a story that requires an element of faith to tell and believe."[59] He would be going out of doubt not out of faith.[60] Faith, Hebrews tells us, is "the assurance of things hoped for, the conviction of things not seen" (Heb 11:1). "Faith guards hope while it sleeps in silence. Faith protects hope from being prematurely forced to display its results and if it cannot, is pounded into bread and not allowed to germinate."[61]

Hope can be longing for something that we will never get, in contrast with hope "in" Jesus Christ. This was made particularly clear by a student of Anderson's who took a course from him while she was in prison. She had hoped for a parole but was turned down. "But I've finally found the concept that clarified this for me. I have too often confused the OBJECT of my hope (the parole) with the SUBJECT of my hope—Christ Jesus. Instead of hoping 'for,' I must hope 'in.' I will not always get what I hope for, but I will never be disappointed by hoping in Christ."[62] Ray Anderson was not ashamed to find theological lessons in some of the most unlikely or less regarded places.

Living by "the seasons of hope," Anderson contends, is embracing all of the different stages of being human, including aging, rather than fighting against them. Does the ministry of the church express this kind of eschatology, which admits our finitude yet still celebrates the present,

55. *SOH*, 14.
56. *SOH*, 23.
57. *SOH*, 120.
58. *SOH*, 54; *UW*, "The Cows Still Stand Up at Midnight on Christmas Eve," 118–24.
59. *SOH*, 54.
60. *UW*, 119.
61. *SOH*, 55.
62. *SOH*, 80.

which respects, in Bonhoeffer's terms, the penultimate as well as the ultimate? Anderson believes that embracing our finitude and our limitations is the message of the book of Ecclesiastes, not skepticism and cynicism.[63] "Apparently, we are given just enough insight to gain one good look at where we are and who we are, and then the clouds roll in and the drapes are pulled and we are not permitted to see as much as God sees."[64] Our tragedy is that we know that is the case.[65] But what are we to do with that knowledge? This is Ecclesiastes' wisdom. If Ecclesiastes is a skeptic then "he is skeptical of a life that forgets that it is destined for death. . . . He is skeptical of a happiness which forgets its time limit. . . . He is skeptical of any joy that does not encompass sadness."[66] Kierkegaard speaks of living in "the eleventh hour."[67] Anderson paraphrases him in this way: "From the perspective of the eleventh hour, there is no such thing as youth and old age. For the sins of youth are not so much the missteps of the young person as they are the presumption of the person who refuses to live life as though it were the eleventh hour. This is not only true of young people."[68]

Ecclesiastes' declarations of "Vanity! vanity!" are declarations of hope (Eccl 1:2), but not hope in a prolonged earthly existence. "The vanity of life is its hope."[69] Death is a part of "the seasons of hope" but that does not deny its tragedy. "Death is part of the sadness of life but it is also a part of the reality of life."[70] Ecclesiastes realizes that temporal life promises more than it gives. "He sees the lack of love between family members, the lack of concern for the well-being of others. And seeing all of this, he becomes terribly wise, but dreadfully sad, for he sees too much that's crooked and cannot be straightened."[71] Something is missing, he realizes. In recognizing that vanity there is hope for something more.[72] "Death is unavoidable, for it is a part of life; it is the end of the beginning. But the human spirit can neither be encompassed by a beginning nor by an end, and the heart

63. *EIG.*
64. *EIG*, 11.
65. *EIG*, 13.
66. *EIG*, 16.
67. Kierkegaard, *The Journals of Kierkegaard*, 76.
68. *EIG*, 85.
69. *EIG*, 20.
70. *EIG*, 89.
71. *EIG*, 29.
72. *EIG*, 26.

knows it."[73] The answer is not to cleave to that which we possess. That is only a recipe for anxiety. "Anxiety robs us of the joy of the things that we possess by anticipating their loss."[74]

Is not our temptation either to restrict hope to an existence after death or to expect nothing but ease because we in effect believe that the kingdom has "come," that God affirms only the status quo? Respecting "the seasons of hope" teaches us otherwise. That is what I believe Anderson is getting at by "the seasons of hope." It is a call to see the ministry of Jesus Christ as recognizing that Christ, by coming into the present from the future, does not obliterate the present, but sanctifies it. Each one of these "seasons" we live in is holy, including death. So spiritual disciplines like prayer and meditation on the Scriptures, are not just to be practiced for their own sake; that would be only bodybuilding, not the exercise that trains you for the game. Exercise is that which prepares you for the future.[75] "When we live by the rhythm of the seasons we are kept from plunging directly from the long summer days into the winter's long night."[76]

Anderson cites Ernest Becker, the author of *The Denial of Death*, as one who demonstrates that death penetrates into every aspect of our lives.[77] Against Freud, it is not sex but the denial that we are going to die that is the chief motivating factor in life. Even in our "heroic projects" we are motivated by that which we are not going to escape: our death. We are constantly, therefore, trying to prove that we are gods. Based on Kierkegaard's view of anxiety, Anderson recognizes the "penetrating insight" of Becker but sees his failure in his individualistic concept of the person and the emptiness of his theological core.[78] Nonetheless, Anderson recognizes how important it is for the Christian, and one's theological anthropology, to come to terms with the real person. The question is agonizing but imperative to Anderson's theological anthropology: "How can I have continuity of my being when my place of belonging and my community of fellow human beings can be so impermanent and so transitory?"[79]

---

73. *EIG*, 89.
74. *EIG*, 59.
75. *SOH*, 151.
76. *SOH*, 135.
77. Becker, *The Denial of Death*.
78. *TDD*, 29–31.
79. *OBH*, 176.

There is no virtue in resorting to the doctrine of the immortality of the soul too quickly.[80] Anderson's understanding of humanity as co-humanity cannot be ignored. "There is something inherently tragic about the form of our present community of human love. We have presence to each other only through the present reality of discontinuity. No other person is ever totally 'at hand' to us. Even if it should appear to be so in any given moment, there is an inevitability of separation and distance which each person must traverse. Everyone experiences (if that is the correct word) death as an 'I' and not as a 'we.' Even during extended and pervasive illness, the presence-in-absence becomes more acute."[81]

Again, it is real, actual persons whom Christ ministers to in his incarnate and continuing ministry, not idealized and spiritualized ones. Yet "presence-in-absence" is a reality that we also know from the giving of the Holy Spirit as the "presence-in-absence" of the resurrected Christ in the church. Co-humanity as community only prepares us to participate in that reality. "Yet this limit does not become fatal because God also promises to uphold the human person through that natural limit through a personal and spiritual relation with Himself."[82] This is neither glory in nor Stoic acceptance in death for the Christian. "Death is not a limiting concept which gives meaning to life; rather the meaning of death must be found in the meaning of the death of Jesus Christ."[83] Anderson does not leave his incarnational theology behind when it comes to death and dying. A theology of the real and continuing presence of Christ must be able to deal with and live with that which speaks of absence and loss. Jesus as the *eschatos*, "the last one" brings the eschaton as "the significance of the self."[84] He is the final word that comes from the future into the present. That is where ministry takes place now, even the continuing ministry of Jesus Christ, not in our capacity to hope.[85] The Holy Spirit is the "presence in absence" of the resurrected Christ.[86] "Death is no mere abstraction, nor can it be made meaningful as an abstract concept. There must be meaning

---

80. *OBH*, 177.
81. *OBH*, 177–78.
82. *TDD*, 49.
83. *TDD*, 11.
84. *OBH*, "Eschaton—The Significance of the Self," 175–78.
85. *OBH*, 176.
86. *OBH*, 176–77.

to death precisely because there must be meaning to each individual's death. It is in the historical life and death of Jesus Christ that Christian theology finds its answer to the meaning of death."[87]

Such a christological approach should not simply be an expression of Christian triumphalism and false optimism. Anderson, instead, sees the implications of Christology for death and dying in their relationship to the Christian community, the body of Christ. Here again we see the importance of the essence of being as co-humanity. In a memorable section of *On Being Human*, Anderson speaks of "Contextualizing Death in a Community of Faith and Hope."[88] Who took the bones of Jacob and Joseph back to the Promised Land after their death? Why was this so important (Gen 47:29–30; 50:24–26)? Because our humanity even in its death is found "contextualized" in community. In this action, something is said by the ancient Hebrews about the significance of the body. At death we are no longer in control of our body; the community needs to take over. (I would say, perform a *vicarious* function!). "It follows from this that the indignity of death is the loss of the use of the body. Dying involves an approaching disjunction between the body and soul at the functional level, not the theoretical level. Thus, death is a final indignity because the body becomes a mere object over which the person has no control."[89]

The place of the community in the context of the dying has profound ethical implications. "The community—whether represented by the congregation of God's people or a family, or a friend, or the lover of the one who has died—must assume subjective responsibility for the body in the death of a person. To allow the body to become a mere impersonal object is to commit an indignity against the person."[90]

Community, like in a New Orleans funeral, is a *processional* that is a part of the person's *pilgrimage*. "Dying is meant to be contextualized in the form of a processional. Death is not an end, but the transition to a new beginning. To die without a processional which manifests that transition through the presence of a human community under the power of the divine Word is to be abandoned at the moment when one is weakest and most vulnerable."[91] Therefore, the community must not simply

---

87. *TDD*, 11.
88. *OBH*, 140–45.
89. *OBH*, 142.
90. *OBH*, 142.
91. *OBH*, 143.

surrender the body of a person to the professional that can dispose of it. "And so, that which is *professional* in the service of burying the dead must be continually contextualized by that which is *processional*."[92] The community of the processional is giving that person over to God. "We who are a subjective community of human existence give over the person to another community of divine fellowship. When we let go of the hand we do so with the deepest conviction of our souls that without faltering or fumbling someone else is taking that hand."[93] Despite the advances of medical technology, even a routine operation can have a tragic end, as Anderson relates concerning a former parishioner who "died in a year's agonizing, prolonged, and unrelenting suffering. All that could be done by the people who loved her was to make out of that entire year a processional of companionship and communion in faith, a manifestation of presence, one to another and both to God."[94] In like manner, the women came to the tomb to anoint the body of Jesus, "not as professionals who had learned how to mask the reality of death from the eyes of the living, but as those who know that the dead need the living to hold them in community."[95] Anderson has returned to "lived transcendence," the real presence of Christ that continues in the church through the Spirit.

There is a Christian perspective not only on death but also on dying, Anderson is saying. "There is no way to acquire an absolutely precise insight into the mystery of death."[96] Near death experiences are common. Medical ethics questions abound concerning the moment of death. We do not yet know what it means to experience death but we can know what it means to approach death. Anderson's story of his own father's death is telling. During a prolonged struggle with cancer, his father "never expressed bitterness about dying at a relatively young age. He voiced no regret and did not protest against the unfairness of it all."[97] Anderson re-

92. *OBH*, 143.

93. *OBH*, 143.

94. *OBH*, 143. In writing this chapter I cannot help but think of the similarity between Ray Anderson's theology and the fiction of the Kentucky farmer Wendell Berry. In Berry's fictional community of Port William you find people that live the ordinary yet extraordinary "membership" that Ray Anderson speaks of as co-humanity. In a way, Berry's fiction "fleshes out" the theology of Ray Anderson, and I think Ray saw that (see *SOG* on Berry's *Jayber Crow*, 164–65, 199–200).

95. *OBH*, 144.

96. *OBH*, 144.

97. *UW*, 108–9.

Ministry as the Future of Christ Coming into the Present

members a Sunday afternoon stroll through the community cemetery. His father did not say much but what he said was revealing: "Yes, and here is the two-year-old Peterson boy. He was kicked in the head by a cow and died that very night."[98] There was no complaining to God or questioning the fairness of that death. "What did he think about when he pulled weeds from the plot where he himself would someday be buried? Did he have anxiety? Did he fear that death would destroy all of the meaning of his life"[99] "I don't know," Anderson muses. "He never said. Death and God were the two subjects never openly questioned. Both were assumed to be beyond doubt and, therefore, beyond question."[100] Is this an example of Kierkegaard's "unconscious despair," the despair of not knowing you are in despair, a despair more insidious than conscious despair?[101] Or does Anderson see this as a picture of Ernest Becker's "heroic projects" in his book *The Denial of Death,* projects that we create in order to deny the fact that we are going to die?[102] Interestingly enough, he provides a different interpretation of his father.

In contrast to our culture of entitlement and complaint, Anderson offers the example of his father as one who did not base his response to the end of life on lament but acceptance. This is not to rule out lament, for even Jesus lamented in Gethsemane (Luke 22:42; Mark 14:34). Yet Jesus also lived in obedience to the Father, "living so that death is not a defeat," in Anderson's words.[103] "I live with the certainty of my own death. My death, I suppose, will be a loss for those who love me, and I can even speak of it as a loss of my own life. But it can never be a defeat. I am not in a 'life-and-death' struggle, in which death can rob me of some hoped-for victory or prize."[104]

What Anderson is speaking of here is his theology of "the seasons of hope," the title of one of his last books. "What is a fair share of life? The only share that I have is what I have been given. Life cannot be measured by its length, as though I have earned some right to a long life. Nor can it

---

98. *UW*, 112.
99. *UW*, 112.
100. *UW*, 112.
101. Kierkegaard, *The Sickness Unto Death*, 42–47.
102. Becker, *The Denial of Death*, 159ff.
103. *UW*, 113.
104. *UW*, 113.

be measured by the amount of goods and money I can amass, as though such things somehow broadened or deepened my 'share of life.'"[105] The entirety of life needs to be seen as something given, as grace. Here is where "the mystery of death is intimately connected to the miracle of birth. Each is a gift."[106] The farmer, like Anderson's father, more readily sees this as one contemplates sowing and harvest through the different seasons of the year. "But for every death there was also a birth. My father witnessed birth each year as the seeds he had sown burst into green and growing life."[107] Recognizing the seasons of life helps us to see certain "rhythms" in life, "letting the rhythm of life carry some of the risk."[108] Here is human life as co-humanity again, for these rhythms are recognized by communities.

> Our existence is not an isolated series of individual episodes taking place as points in time. Rather, life involves us in a common pilgrimage. At any given time, we are part of a community where birth and death, joy and sorrow, pain and pleasure, as well as sowing and harvest are taking place. These communal experiences are the rhythms, the seasonal cycles, of life. For every milestone in our life—birth, love, marriage, failure, sadness, death—there is a pulse in the life of the human family. This collective rhythm is meant to help carry the risk of each person's existence.[109]

This is "living so that death is not a surprise"![110] One wonders how my baby boom generation, with all of our sense of entitlement and narcissism, will respond to our increasing aging in the years ahead! Will we possess the resources to age, even to die, with grace?

Anderson's father was silent during his final hours. Yet when the Lutheran minister spoke the words of the twenty-third Psalm, his father responded. "At the sound of his voice my father, who had not moved for hours, moved his hands and folded them on his breast. This was an incredible sign of the fact that, while we had given up attempting to communicate with him, he was a person in whom the Word of God could provoke and summon forth a response of hearing."[111] His family was there

105. *UW*, 114.
106. *UW*, 110.
107. *UW*, 110.
108. *UW*, 84.
109. *UW*, 85.
110. *UW*, 111.
111. *OBH*, 145; *UW*, 109.

to take care of him in processional as he was summoned by the Word of God. The God who became human is present in a very human place; choosing to be present, not abstractly, not "spiritually," but in the community. "There is co-humanity, even in the process of dying. The eschatological reality of the resurrection of the body is grasped from this side of life and the divine Word which sustains the human person in unity of body and soul is manifest."[112] This is the kind of hope that can legitimately be healthy-minded because it is the hope based on the resurrection of the "flesh and bones" of Jesus: "See my hands and feet, that it is I myself; handle me, and see; for a spirit has not flesh and bones as you see that I have" (Luke 24:38–39).

A Case Study to Consider: "Death"[113]

Facts and Dilemma

Jean (not her real name), a nurse, was preparing for the day's surgery schedule and checked the paper work on the donor tissue for corneal transplants. She noted an eighteen year old male, abdominal wound, a twenty-seven year old female, motor vehicle accident, a forty-seven year old male, myocardial infarction, and a fifty-four year old male, pulmonary embolus, as the causes of death. She could reassure all of her patients that they were receiving young, healthy tissue.

That evening she called on her cousin Teresa who was diagnosed with colon cancer two years ago. Following surgery, the cancer metastasized to the liver and she received chemo and radiation until her platelets dropped to critical levels. She waited for seven months for her platelets to increase before the liver resection. This was a difficult time and she reached out to a charismatic church for prayer and laying on of hands. She is from a devout Catholic family and this caused some confusion for her parents and husband. However, they supported her in whatever she needed to keep her hopes up. She has now developed fluid in the abdomen and goes to the hospital once a week to get the fluid drained;

---

112. *OBH*, 145.

113. This case study was provided by Laurinda Wade, a graduate student in ministry at Friends University.

medically, this is not a good sign. Friends and family have avoided discussing death with her. Jean wonders: is it a gift or a burden to have time to prepare for death?

About a month ago Jean's church requested members to distribute flyers in the neighborhood. It was an outreach to let them know who we were and the activities at the church. We were not asked to knock on the doors but to visit with people if we had the opportunity. Matt, the assistant pastor, handed Jean the flyers and she asked, "What do I say if they ask me about the resurrection body and heaven?" There was dead silence until we all just had to laugh. Finally, he said, "Those of us who are introverts just roll them up and stick them in the door."

Meditating on her own death for several years, Jean has an awareness of her own physical mortality as one breath away. However, the little she understands about immortality she has picked up from attending funerals. She has heard more teachings from 1 Corinthians chapter 15 on the resurrection than any other scripture in the Bible. It is such a beautiful promise of eternal life and hope that she naturally thought it would be the first topic people would want to ask me about the church. Jean asks her pastor, "Does my life experience define eternal life or does God?"

What are the implications of these thoughts from Anderson in responding to Jean?

Questions to Ponder

1. "I wonder what church Jesus would like to visit if he suddenly returned to earth?" the student asked Anderson. Does this have any implications for issues of death and afterlife?

2. In the book of Acts "we see that the emerging church in Antioch, which came out of the future by virtue of the Spirit of Christ gathering and baptizing both Jew and Gentile into the body of Christ, accepted, affirmed, and claimed to be part of the community of Christ at Jerusalem. The Jerusalem church did not reciprocate." What does it mean for the church to "come out of the future"? Does this say anything about death and afterlife?

Ministry as the Future of Christ Coming into the Present

3. Concerning election: "God has taken himself the fate of eternal estrangement and so removed death as an obstacle to the possibility of redemption of all." Does this imply universalism?

4. "How far was Jesus sent into the world?" Did he go into the depths of even Judas' hell?

5. A comment on a suicide: "This man placed himself outside of God's grace by taking his own life?" How does Anderson respond to this?

6. On "the middle zone": "To project what we know as truly 'human' backward into sheer biological material may be to think beyond what we actually know and border on the absurd. In the same way, to project what we know as truly 'human' forward into some kind of post mortal form of life can become equally absurd."

7. The student of Anderson's who was in prison: "I have too often confused the OBJECT of my hope (the parole) with the SUBJECT of my hope—Christ Jesus. Instead of hoping 'for,' I must hope 'in.' I will not always get what I hope for, but I will never be disappointed by hoping in Christ."

8. On Ecclesiastes: If the author of Ecclesiastes is a skeptic then "he is skeptical of a life that forgets that it is destined for death. . . . He is skeptical of a happiness which forgets its time limit. . . . He is skeptical of any joy that does not encompass sadness."

9. "There is something inherently tragic about the form of our present community of human love. . . . Everyone experiences (if that is the correct word) death as an 'I' and not as a 'we.' Even during extended and pervasive illness, the presence-in-absence becomes more acute."

10. "Dying is meant to be contextualized in the form of a processional. Death is not an end, but the transition to a new beginning. To die without a processional which manifests that transition through the presence of a human community under the power of the divine Word is to be abandoned at the moment when one is weakest and most vulnerable."

11. "I live with the certainty of my own death. My death, I suppose, will be a loss for those who love me, and I can even speak of it as a loss of

my own life. But it can never be a defeat. I am not in a 'life-and-death' struggle, in which death can rob me of some hoped-for victory or prize."

12. "Our existence is not an isolated series of individual episodes taking place as points in time. Rather, life involves us in a common pilgrimage. At any given time, we are part of a community where birth and death, joy and sorrow, pain and pleasure, as well a sowing and harvest are taking place."

BIBLIOGRAPHY

Anderson, Ray S. *Christians Who Counsel: The Vocation of Wholistic Therapy*. Grand Rapids: Zondervan, 1990.

———. "Christopraxis: Competence as a Criterion for Theological Education." *TSF Bulletin* (Jan–Feb, 1984) 10-13.

———. *Dancing with Wolves while Feeding the Sheep: Musings of a Maverick Theologian*. 2000. Reprint. Eugene, OR: Wipf and Stock, 2002.

———. *Don't Give Up On Me—I'm Not Finished Yet: Putting the Finishing Touches on the Person You Want to Be*. New York: McCracken, 1994.

———. *An Emerging Theology for an Emerging Church*. Downers Grove, IL: InterVarsity, 2006.

———. *Everything That Makes Me Happy I Learned When I Grew Up*. Downers Grove, IL: InterVarsity, 1995.

———. *Exploration into God: Sermonic Meditations on the Book of Ecclesiastes*. Eugene, OR: Wipf and Stock, 2006.

———. *The Gospel according to Judas*. Colorado Springs: Helmers & Howard, 1991.

———. *Historical Transcendence and the Reality of God*. Grand Rapids: Eerdmans, 1975.

———. *Judas and Jesus: Amazing Grace for the Wounded Soul*. Eugene, OR: Cascade, 2005.

———. Letter (response to Mouw, Brown, and Muller, "Now That the Party Is Over: Was Karl that Good?"). *Reformed Journal* 37 (May, 1987) 6–8.

———. *Like Living Stones*. Minneapolis: Free Church, 1964.

———. *Living the Spiritually Balanced Life: Acquiring the Virtues You Admire*. Grand Rapids: Baker, 1998.

———. *Minding God's Business*. Grand Rapids: Eerdmans, 1986. Revised edition, Eugene, OR: Wipf & Stock, 2008.

———. *Ministry on the Fireline: A Practical Theology for an Empowered Church*. Downers Grove, IL: InterVarsity, 1993.

———. *The New Age of Soul: Spiritual Wisdom for a New Millenium*. Eugene, OR: Wipf & Stock, 2000.

Bibliography

———— and Dennis B. Guernsey. *On Being Family: A Social Theology of the Family.* Grand Rapids: Eerdmans, 1985.

————. *On Being Human: Essays in Theological Anthropology.* Grand Rapids: Eerdmans, 1982.

————. "The Practical Theology of Thomas F. Torrance." *Participatio: Journal of the Thomas F. Torrance Theological Fellowship* 1 (2009). On-line: http://www.tftorrance.org.

————. *The Seasons of Hope: Empowering Faith through the Practice of Hope.* Eugene, OR: Wipf & Stock, 2008.

————. *Self-Care: A Theology of Personal Empowerment and Spiritual Healing.* Wheaton, IL: Bridgepoint, 1995.

————. *The Shape of Practical Theology: Empowering Ministry with Theological Praxis.* Downers Grove, IL: InterVarsity, 2001.

————. *Something Old, Something New: Marriage and Family Ministry in a Postmodern Culture.* Eugene, OR: Wipf & Stock, 2007.

————. *The Soul of God: A Theological Memoir.* Eugene, OR: Wipf & Stock, 2004.

————. *The Soul of Ministry: Forming Leaders for God's People.* Louisville: Westminster/John Knox, 1997.

————. *Soulprints: Personal Reflections on Faith, Hope, and Love.* Huntington Beach, CA: Ray S. Anderson, 1996.

————. *Spiritual Caregiving as Secular Sacrament: A Practical Theology for Professional Caregivers.* New York: Jessica Kingsley, 2003.

————. "Theological Anthropology." In *The Blackwell Companion to Modern Theology*, edited by Gareth Jones, 82–94. Malden, MA: Blackwell, 2004.

————, editor. *Theological Foundations for Ministry.* Edinburgh: T. & T. Clark, 1979.

————. *Theology, Death, and Dying.* Oxford: Blackwell, 1986.

————. "Toward a Holistic Psychology: Putting All the Pieces in their Proper Place." *Edification: Journal of the Society for Christian Psychology* 1 (2007) 5–16.

————. *Unspoken Wisdom: Truths My Father Taught Me.* Minneapolis: Fortress, 1995.

Barth, Karl. *Church Dogmatics.* Edited by T. F. Torrance and G. W. Bromiley. Edinburgh: T. & T. Clark, 1936–69.

————. *Dogmatics in Outline.* Translated by G. T. Thomson. New York: Philosophical Library, 1949.

————. *Evangelical Theology: An Introduction.* Translated by Grover Foley. New York: Holt, Rinehart and Winston, 1963.

————. *God Here and Now.* Translated by Paul M. van Buren. New York: Harper & Row, 1964.

————. *The Humanity of God.* Translated by Thomas Wieser. Atlanta: John Knox, 1960.

Becker, Ernest. *The Denial of Death.* New York: Free Press, 1973.

Berkouwer, G. C. *The Sacraments.* Translated by Hugo Bekker. Grand Rapids: Eerdmans, 1969.

Berry, Wendell. *Jayber Crow.* Washington, DC: Counterpoint, 2000.

Bonhoeffer, Dietrich. *Ethics.* Dietrich Bonhoeffer Works, 6. Edited by Clifford J. Green. Translated by Reinhard Krauss, et al. Minneapolis: Fortress, 2005.

————. *Letters and Papers from Prison.* New Greatly Enlarged Edition. Edited by Eberhard Bethge. New York: Macmillan, 1972.

————. *Sanctorum Communio: A Theological Study of the Sociology of the Church.* Edited by Clifford J. Green. Translated by Reinhard Krauss and Nancy Lukens. Dietrich Bonhoeffer Works 2. Minneapolis: Fortress, 1998.

Bibliography

Bowmer, John. *The Sacrament of the Lord's Supper in Early Methodism.* London: Dacre, 1951.

Brown, Warren S., Nancey Murphy, and H. Newton Malony, editors. *Whatever Happened to the Soul? Scientific and Theological Portraits of Human Nature.* Minneapolis: Fortress, 1998.

Calvin, John. *Institutes of the Christian Religion.* Edited by John T. McNeill. Translated by Ford Lewis Battles. Philadelphia: Westminster, 1960.

Carnell, Edward J. *Christian Commitment: An Apologetic.* New York: Macmillan, 1957.

Childs, Brevard S. *Biblical Theology of the Old and New Testaments: Theological Reflection on the Christian Bible.* Minneapolis: Fortress, 1992.

Clark, Tony. *Divine Revelation and Human Practice.* Eugene, OR: Cascade, 2008.

Cobb, John B., Jr., and David Ray Griffin. *Process Theology: An Introductory Exposition.* Philadelphia: Westminster, 1976.

Dawson, Gerrit. *Jesus Ascended: The Meaning of Christ's Continuing Incarnation.* Phillipsburg, NJ: P. & R., 2004.

The Dark Knight. Directed by Christopher Nolan. Warner Bros. Pictures, 2008.

Ford, David F. *The Modern Theologians.* 2nd ed. Oxford: Blackwell, 1997.

Gunton, Colin E., editor. *The Cambridge Companion to Christian Doctrine.* Cambridge: Cambridge University Press, 1997.

Hart, David Bentley. "Where Was God? An Interview with David Bentley Hart." *Christian Century* 123 (January, 2006) 26–29.

Hauerwas, Stanley. "On Doctrine and Ethics." In *The Cambridge Companion to Christian Doctrine*, edited by Colin E. Gunton, 21–40. Cambridge: Cambridge University Press, 1997.

Jones, Gareth, editor. *The Blackwell Companion to Modern Theology.* Malden, MA: Blackwell, 2004.

Kettler, Christian D. *The God Who Believes: Faith, Doubt, and the Vicarious Humanity of Christ.* Eugene, OR: Cascade, 2005.

——— and Todd H. Speidell, editors. *Incarnational Ministry: The Presence of Christ in Church, Society, and Family: Essays in Honor of Ray S. Anderson.* Colorado Springs: Helmers & Howard, 1990.

Kierkegaard, Søren. *The Journals of Kierkegaard.* Translated by Alexander Dru. New York: Harper Torchbooks, 1959.

———. *The Sickness unto Death.* Edited and translated by Howard V. Hong and Edna H. Hong. Princeton University Press, 1980.

Lewis, John P. "The Formative Influence of Karl Barth in the Theology of Ray S. Anderson." *Colloquim* 37 (2005) 27–44.

———. *Karl Barth in North America: The Influence of Karl Barth in the Making of a New North American Evangelicalism.* Eugene, OR: Resource, 2009.

Lindsell, Harold. *The Bible in the Balance.* Grand Rapids: Eerdmans, 1979.

Marsden, George. *Reforming Fundamentalism: Fuller Seminary and the New Evangelicalism.* Grand Rapids: Eerdmans, 1987.

Mouw, Richard, Colin Brown, and Richard Muller. "Now That the Party Is Over: Was Karl Barth That Good?" *Reformed Journal* 37 (1987) 16–22.

Pearson, William L. *Notes on the Sacraments.* Cleveland: William G. Hubbard, 1888.

Pinnock, Clark, et al. *The Openness of God: A Biblical Challenge to the Traditional Understanding of God.* Downers Grove, IL: InterVarsity, 1994.

Bibliography

Polanyi, Michael. *Personal Knowledge: Towards a Post-Critical Philosophy.* Chicago: University of Chicago Press, 1958.

———. *The Tacit Dimension.* Garden City, NY: Doubleday, 1967.

Speidell, Todd, editor. *On Being Christian . . . and Human: Essays in Celebration of Ray S. Anderson.* Eugene, OR: Wipf & Stock, 2002.

Surin, Kenneth. *The Turnings of Darkness and Light: Essays in Philosophical and Systematic Theology.* Cambridge: Cambridge University Press, 1989.

Thiselton, Anthony C. *The Two Horizons: New Testament Hermeneutics and Philosophical Description.* Grand Rapids: Eerdmans, 1980.

Thorne, Phillip R. *Evangelicalism and Karl Barth: His Reception and Influence in North American Evangelical Theology.* Princeton Theological Monograph Series 40. Allison Park, PA: Pickwick, 1995.

Torrance, James B. "Strengths and Weaknesses of the Westminster Theology." In *The Westminster Confession in the Church Today*, edited by Alasdair I. C. Heron, 40–54. Edinburgh: Saint Andrew Press, 1982.

———. "The Unconditional Freeness of Grace." *Theological Renewal* 9 (1978) 7–14.

Torrance, T. F. *The Christian Doctrine of God: One Being, Three Persons.* Edinburgh: T. & T. Clark, 1996.

———. *Divine and Contingent Order.* Oxford: Oxford University Press, 1981.

———. *Theology in Reconciliation: Essays Towards Evangelical and Catholic Unity in East and West.* Grand Rapids: Eerdmans, 1975.

———. *The Mediation of Christ.* Rev. ed. Colorado Springs: Helmers & Howard, 1992.

———. *Scottish Theology: From John Knox to John McLeod Campbell.* Edinburgh: T. & T. Clark, 1996.

———. *Space, Time, and Resurrection.* Grand Rapids: Eerdmans, 1976.

———. *The Trinitarian Faith: The Evangelical Theology of the Ancient Catholic Church.* Edinburgh: T. & T. Clark, 1988.

Trueblood, D. Elton. *The People Called Quakers.* New York: Harper & Row, 1966.

Wainwright, Geoffrey. "Letters to the Editor." *TSF Bulletin* (Sept–Oct, 1984) 2.

Watson, Francis. "Hermeneutics." In *The Cambridge Companion to Christian Doctrine*, edited by Colin E. Gunton, 65–80. Cambridge: Cambridge University Press, 1997.

Wesley, John. *The Journal of the Rev. John Wesley, A.M.* Vol. 2. Edited by Nehemiah Curnock, 1738–42. London: Kelly, n.d.

Williams, Rowan. Review of *Historical Transcendence and the Reality of God*, by Ray S. Anderson. *Downside Review* 94 (1976) 236–39.

Wood, Ralph C. *The Comedy of Redemption: Christian Faith and Comic Vision in Four American Novelists.* Notre Dame, IN: University of Notre Dame Press, 1988.

Young, Peter M., VI. "The Ontological Self in the Thinking of C. Stephen Evans and Ray S. Anderson." PhD diss., Fuller Theological Seminary, 1991.

Zizioulas, John D. *Communion and Otherness: Further Studies in Personhood and the Church.* Edited by Paul McPartlan. London: T. & T. Clark, 2006.

———. "Human Capacity and Human Incapacity: A Theological Exploration of Personhood." *Scottish Journal of Theology* 28 (1975) 401–47.

www.ingramcontent.com/pod-product-compliance
Lightning Source LLC
Chambersburg PA
CBHW051742230426
43670CB00012B/2120